Entertaining on Ice

Entertaining on Ice

Short-term freezing for the busy cook

Tessa Hayward

Photographs by Michelle Garrett

Kyle Cathie Ltd

First published in Great Britain 1998 by
Kyle Cathie Limited
20 Vauxhall Bridge Road
London SW1V 2SA

10 9 8 7 6 5 4 3 2 1

ISBN 1 85626 291 X

A Cataloguing In Publication record for this title is available from the British Library.

Edited by Sophie Bessemer
Copy-edited by Stephanie Horner
Home economy by Susie Theodorou, assisted by Belinda Keating
Designed by harperpeel design
Production by Lorraine Baird
Typeset by SX Composing

Colour reproduction by Chromagraphics (Overseas) Pte. Ltd, Singapore
Printed and bound in Singapore by Tien Wah Press

Photograph on page 2 shows Salmon with Salsa Verde (page 56) and
Salmon with Salsa Rossa (page 57).

Contents

Acknowledgements

So many friends have been kind and given me ideas, suggestions and often complete recipes. I would like to thank them all, and especially those named below, for their great generosity which has been much appreciated:
Erica Austen, Jane Barne, Gisella Clanmorris, Isabelle Erroll, Susie Hilleary, Cazzie Kaye, Anne Minoprio, Marie-Pierre Moine, Lavinia Seymour, Gillian Sladen and Teresa Wallace.

I would also like to thank Kyle Cathie and her team for giving me the opportunity to write the book which has, for the most part, been a very enjoyable exercise.

My thanks and appreciation also to my agent, Jane Conway-Gordon, for being so helpful and supportive.

introduction

Last summer we went to spend a country weekend with some friends. It was beautifully sunny and we had a most enjoyable time with delicious food and wine and with people constantly coming and going.

Throughout the activity our hostess always seemed to be present and remained looking totally calm and collected. I eventually discovered her secret – she was a wizard with the deep freeze and many of the dishes she produced had been made a week or two ahead, or just a few days earlier, and stored in her freezer. There is nothing dramatically new in using the deep freeze for dishes you've cooked but recently I feel it seems to have been pushed to one side by the thought that nothing need take more than half an hour to prepare and that the main use for the freezer is to store and keep fresh food or ready-cooked bought food for busy times. A good concept, except that when all members of the family are together or friends are invited I like to give them home-cooked food. Importantly, I also want to see them and enjoy their company so time spent alone in the kitchen is time wasted.

After our happy weekend I returned to my half-forgotten freezer and it was a revelation. The next time we entertained, and long before the doorbell went, the cooking was done, the saucepans and bowls were all washed up and

back in the cupboard and the food – starters, casseroles, vegetables, tarts or whatever – was slowly defrosting in the fridge.

Since then I've cooked constantly for my freezer and I've broken away from the image that home-frozen food means rather heavy casseroles or over-thick soups and this book is the result. There is no reason why the fresh-tasting ingredients we all relish nowadays should not be incorporated into a light sauce and the dish then frozen for a week or two before it's due to be consumed.

Using this book

All the recipes here have been chosen because they are freezer-friendly and because they need very little attention after defrosting. As you try out the recipes, you will find that any additional work that does need to be done after defrosting is detailed in the right-hand column. Many require no more effort than being put into the oven to reheat or even being unwrapped and placed on a serving plate; others just a quick finishing touch such as a scattering of pinenuts. So you can entertain without having to cook: literally have your (home-made) cake and eat it. For those that do need a little more work

on the day you'll find any additional ingredients clearly listed in the left-hand column. Please note however that any serving suggestion I give is purely that – no more than an accompaniment that strikes me as appropriate – so no particular ingredients are given for these. Feel free to vary (and ignore!) such suggestions as you wish.

None of the dishes is difficult or complicated to make. Even when you are cooking ahead, time can be limited so there are recipes for the days when you are in a hurry and others for those days when you feel you can lavish tender loving care on preparing more involved dishes. Many of the recipes are suitable for vegetarians, or can be easily adapted; you'll find the most suitable ones are marked with a **Ⓥ**. Finally, this book is not about fast food but the redistribution of your time so that you can prepare recipes in advance when it suits you. However, do bear in mind that it is not essential to freeze each dish for successful entertaining since any of the recipes in the book work just as well when cooked and eaten from fresh.

I firmly believe you will find this book an invaluable and useful aid in the kitchen. Maybe you will find it necessary to follow my example and go out and buy a second freezer.

For the best results the way food is wrapped and frozen is extremely important, so please, before you start cooking from the book, read the golden rules on freezing.

A note on weights and measures

Now that most food is weighed metrically I think it is time that we all started to cook metrically. However, I do give both metric and imperial measurements. Use one or other but do not mix them. I know that some of the imperial amounts may sound a little odd or uneven but I have used the conversion table set out by the Guild of Food Writers which gives the nearest possible conversions. Scales with weights or modern electronic scales can easily manage the odd $1/2$oz.

Spoonfuls for dry ingredients are rounded and for liquids, obviously, level.

A note on ingredients

Inevitably many of the recipes call for a seasoning of salt and pepper – I have not included these in the ingredients, assuming they will be to hand in any kitchen. Where an unspecified oil is listed as an ingredient, usually for frying, sunflower, vegetable or even olive will do.

Golden rules for freezing

People who live in cold climates have known about preserving food in ice or snow for centuries. Freezing is a totally natural method of preservation as frozen food retains its molecular structure and, provided the food has been properly treated, on defrosting it will be virtually unchanged in both texture and nutritive values. Here are some rules which you must follow to get the best results from freezing.

◆ All food, after careful wrapping, needs to be frozen as quickly as possible - hence the quick-freeze button on modern freezers. During the freezing process, ice crystals form inside the cells of food and it is these crystals that arrest the action of enzymes and bacteria in the food. Provided the food is fast frozen the crystals are very small but if the freezing process is lengthy the ice crystals increase in size and large ones force their way into the cells of the food, causing them to rupture, resulting in loss of both moisture and texture. So it is important that food should be quickly frozen, preferably in a **** freezer. Remember that any cooked food must be left to cool properly before freezing.

◆ When it comes to defrosting, the slower it's done, the better the final texture of the food will be. I know that microwaves are a boon for defrosting but slow defrosting, ideally in the fridge, or on the side in a cool place is what I would recommend for every dish in the book. I have, though, given guidelines to indicate which recipes could be defrosted and reheated or cooked in a microwave, as we are all inclined to forget sometimes to take food from the freezer.

◆ Frozen food also deteriorates relatively quickly and once it has been defrosted it should not be kept for any length of time before it is reheated and eaten. Never re-freeze defrosted food and do check when buying meat, fish or poultry that it has not already been frozen. If it has, you will need to cook it thoroughly before it can be put into your freezer.

◆ It is very important that the food to be frozen should be wrapped properly. I use either foil or a double layer of clingfilm and make absolutely sure that there are no open seams for air to get in. I often suggest using a freezer- and ovenproof casserole or gratin dish which, after defrosting, can go straight into the oven and some types can also be used on the hob. Providing you have room in your freezer and can spare the dish for a week or two, this is much easier and quicker than transferring the prepared food from dish to freezer container and back again. It also saves on washing up, especially those that double as serving dishes, too. Do, however, make sure that the casserole or whatever is tightly covered. (Once a dish comes out of the freezer, I freshly cover it with either tinfoil or cling film, whichever is appropriate.)

◆ Labelling your prepared dishes and keeping a careful list of what goes into the freezer and when is another important stage. It would be easy to confuse two meals in similar containers and, perhaps worse, it would defeat the object of freezing ahead if you kept prepared dishes for longer than they can safely be stored.

◆ Frozen foods keep at optimum quality for different lengths of time but I have not given details as to how many days, weeks or sometimes months each dish in the book can be kept. I see this book as essentially a guide to short-term freezing and cooking ahead for a particular occasion and not cooking to fill up the freezer with dishes for use at some unspecified time in the future. I would not, therefore, recommend that any dish is kept for more than a month.

◆ The use of gelatine in a recipe affects the length of time it can be frozen. Such recipes freeze perfectly well for a couple of weeks but I would not advocate leaving them for longer periods. Gelatine, as you may know, is inclined to break down and turn to water when frozen. I recommend using leaf gelatine which is now quite easy to obtain and preferable as it melts easily and it is not difficult to judge the exact amount needed for any recipe. If you do use powdered gelatine you will need one sachet for every 4 leaves of gelatine; both quantities are sufficient to set 600ml/1 pint of liquid.

◆ A word, too, on flavourings. Many of them, especially onions, garlic, herbs and spices, are apt to re-distribute themselves when frozen and gain in strength so it would be wise to season and spice lightly when cooking for the freezer and to add more, if necessary, after defrosting.

Again, I would not recommend freezing dishes containing garlic or spices for any longer than two, or maybe three, weeks. Although you can, when preparing a recipe, leave out any garlic then add it after defrosting and before reheating.

◆ Many of my recipes are frozen when the meat, poultry or fish are very lightly cooked or, on some occasions, raw and I think the final results merit this treatment. These recipes, in particular, must only be made with fresh meat, poultry or fish and need very careful defrosting and cooking. Follow the instructions and make sure that the meat and poultry are fully cooked, not simply reheated, before serving them.

◆ I have also, where appropriate, noted that dishes can be defrosted and reheated or cooked in a microwave but I have not gone into details as to timings. Microwave ovens

vary greatly in capacity and all come with comprehensive instructions. Do consult the instruction book with your particular model. I also find that timings vary according to the dish used – for instance, food in a thin shallow porcelain dish will heat up much more quickly than the same food in a large thick glass one.

◆ Last but not least, oven temperatures and timings, although given in the recipes, may need to be adjusted according to the dish used and how complete the defrosting has been. A china casserole will heat up quickly but a heavy cast-iron one will take far longer and, if you are using this type, you may find that you need to increase the timings a little. Give some thought before you freeze a dish how it will be reheated or cooked. Metal casseroles, for instance, cannot be used in a microwave, but they can be put on the hob as well as into the oven.

soups & starters

In some ways the first course is the most important one of a meal. It is the springboard for what is to follow and ideally should create interest and expectation and set your tastebuds going. I know that at the ideal party people are busy talking, flirting and enjoying each other's company and I have heard it said that the food is maybe of secondary importance. I think this idea is both sweeping and untrue, as the food and drink each play a part in creating the right ambience for an enjoyable party. The recipes here are very varied, from simple homely soups to a sophisticated terrine, but there is something to suit many different occasions and all times of the year. Cookery books often tell you that when creating a menu and putting a meal together the starter needs careful choosing as it must complement the main course and it must not clash colourwise. I think the question of colour can be overdone, but I do agree that it is often easier to start by deciding on the main course. Having done that you will often find that the choice of starters is whittled down for you, then the final decision becomes easy.

❄ SUMMER SAFFRON, LEEK AND POTATO SOUP ᵛ

Saffron not only gives anything it touches a most beautiful colour but also a most beautiful taste.

SERVES 6

large pinch saffron

4 large leeks, white part only

50g/1³/₄oz butter

250g/9oz floury potatoes, peeled and diced

1.5 litres/2³/₄ pints light chicken or vegetable stock

TO REHEAT OR EAT COLD

300ml/10fl oz whipping cream

handful chervil or parsley, chopped

In a bowl pour a little boiling water over the saffron and let it stand.
◆ Wash the leeks well and slice thinly. Pat dry. Melt the butter in a large pan, add the potatoes and leeks and sauté for 5 minutes, stirring occasionally. Heat the stock and pour it into the pan, then add the saffron and its soaking water. Stir, and bring to the boil. Cover the pan and let it simmer for 20-25 minutes or until the vegetables are really soft.
◆ Drain off and reserve the liquid. Use a food processor or blender to reduce the vegetables to a purée. Return the purée to the reserved liquid and season to taste.

TO FREEZE Pour into a rigid freezer container.

TO DEFROST Leave on the side for 5–6 hours or in the fridge for 15–16 hours.

TO MICROWAVE Follow your microwave instructions for defrosting and reheating.

TO REHEAT Pour the soup into a pan, stir in the cream and season to taste. Stir occasionally while the soup is heating.

TO EAT COLD Stir the soup until smooth, season and pour into bowls. Swirl cream on top and sprinkle with herbs.

❄ SWEET SPANISH ONION AND CIDER SOUP ᵛ

Slowly cooked onions make a sweet-tasting base for this soup. The cider adds bite and the cream gives a velvety texture.

SERVES 6

100g/3¹/₂oz butter

3 medium Spanish onions, peeled and sliced finely

20g/³/₄oz flour

200ml/7fl oz dry cider

1.3 litres/2¹/₄ pints light chicken or vegetable stock

sprig rosemary

TO REHEAT

300ml/10fl oz single cream

handful parsley, chopped

Melt the butter in a large pan and add the onions. Cook over a low heat, stirring occasionally, until they are really soft and yellow. This takes around ³/₄ hour.
◆ Stir in the flour, then the cider and simmer for 3-4 minutes before adding the stock, rosemary and a little salt and pepper. Bring to the boil then simmer for a further 10 minutes. Drain off and reserve the liquid, discard the rosemary and purée the onion in a food processor or blender. Stir the purée back into the liquid.

TO FREEZE Pour into a rigid freezer container.

TO DEFROST Leave on the side for 5–6 hours or overnight in the fridge.

TO MICROWAVE Follow your microwave instructions for defrosting, then add the cream and adjust the seasoning before reheating the soup.

TO REHEAT Heat over a low flame, stirring frequently to prevent the bottom burning. Stir in the cream and adjust the seasoning. Serve sprinkled with parsley over the top.

❄ ITALIAN ROASTED TOMATO AND COURGETTE SOUP ᵛ

A summer soup that sums up good Italian country food. Ripe, aromatic tomatoes are sprinkled with breadcrumbs then baked to concentrate their flavour. The cooked tomato flesh is then added to the shallots and courgettes and everything is frozen. After defrosting the soup is diluted with stock and reheated – very slowly so that the stock takes up all the flavours of the ingredients.

SERVES 6

800g/1lb 12oz ripe, aromatic tomatoes

40g/1¹⁄₂oz fresh breadcrumbs (use ciabatta or a white bread)

1 clove garlic, peeled and finely chopped

3 sprigs tarragon, chopped

2 teaspoons sugar

5 tablespoons olive oil

2 shallots, trimmed and chopped

225g/8oz courgettes, peeled and sliced thickly

TO REHEAT

850ml/1¹⁄₂ pints light chicken or vegetable stock

Preheat the oven to 190°C/375°F/gas 5. Peel the tomatoes, cut them in half and arrange, cut side up, in a roasting tray. Mix the breadcrumbs, garlic, tarragon, sugar and some salt and pepper and sprinkle it on the tomatoes. Drizzle 3 tablespoons of olive oil over the top. Bake the tomatoes for 45 minutes, or until they are soft and starting to blacken round the edges.

◆ Meanwhile, sauté the shallots in the remaining olive oil. When they are soft, add the courgettes and cook until they just start to soften – no more. Remove from the heat and leave to cool.

◆ Add the roasted tomatoes to the onions and courgettes. Pour a little water into the roasting tin to deglaze and scrape up any caramelised bits from the bottom of the tray and add them to the cooked vegetables.

TO FREEZE **Turn into a freezer-proof jar or container.**

TO DEFROST **Leave overnight in the fridge or on the side for 7–8 hours.**

TO MICROWAVE **Follow your microwave instructions for defrosting and reheating.**

TO REHEAT **Turn the soup into a pan, stir in the stock and adjust the seasonings. Bring slowly to a simmer, stirring frequently. Serve the soup immediately or the courgettes will become overcooked and soft.**

❄ PEA, PEAR AND WATERCRESS SOUP ᵛ

An unusual combination that makes a truly special starter. The peas benefit from the sweetness of the pears, which also provide a subtle, illusive flavour. Aim to select fairly ripe, juicy pears, but do try to catch them before they go soft. I make it with Comice but any variety can be used.

SERVES 6–8

75g/2³/₄oz butter

I large onion, chopped

500g/1lb 2oz pears (Comice, if available), peeled, cored and roughly chopped

450g/1lb frozen peas

2 litres/3¹/₂ pints light chicken or vegetable stock

bunch watercress, picked over

Melt the butter in a large pan and cook the onion until very soft. Stir in the pear, cook for a minute or so, then add the peas followed by the stock and the watercress and season lightly. Bring the soup to the boil and simmer for 10 minutes.

◆ Remove from the heat and drain and reserve most of the liquid. Purée the vegetables in a food processor or blender, and then push them through a sieve back into the reserved liquid. Season to taste.

TO FREEZE **Turn the soup into rigid freezer containers.**

TO DEFROST **Leave on the side for 5–6 hours or overnight in the fridge.**

TO MICROWAVE **Follow your microwave instructions for defrosting and reheating.**

TO REHEAT **Reheat slowly in a pan, stirring frequently.**

TO EAT COLD **After defrosting, push it all through a sieve again to return the soup to its original smooth state.**

❄ RED PEPPER AND CELERY SOUP ᵛ

You can eat this soup hot or cold; I use butter if it is destined to be eaten hot and oil if cold.

SERVES 6

4 tablespoons olive oil or 50g/1³/₄oz butter and 1 tablespoon cooking oil

2–3 red peppers, cored, deseeded and chopped

1 large celery heart, washed and sliced

1 Spanish onion, peeled and chopped

400g/14oz can tomatoes

3 sprigs thyme, 1 bay leaf

1.3 litres/2¹/₄ pints light chicken or vegetable stock

Heat the olive oil, or butter and oil, in a large pan, add the fresh vegetables and sauté over a low heat for 15-20 minutes. Stir occasionally and don't let them brown - add a little more oil if necessary. Add the tomatoes and herbs and stir. Cook for a further 5 minutes before adding the stock. Bring it all to simmering point and let it bubble gently for ¹/₂ hour or until the vegetables are cooked.

◆ Strain off and reserve the liquid, discard the bay leaf and thyme. Put the vegetables into a food processor or blender and reduce to a purée. Press the purée through a sieve back into the reserved liquid and season to taste.

TO FREEZE **Pour into rigid freezer containers.**

TO DEFROST **Leave on the side for 5–6 hours or overnight in the fridge.**

TO MICROWAVE **Follow your microwave instructions for defrosting and reheating.**

TO REHEAT **If serving the soup hot reheat it in a pan on the hob.**

TO EAT COLD **Stir the defrosted soup thoroughly.**

❄ CHILLED CURRY MANGO SOUP ⱽ

This is the perfect soup to be eaten outside in the gloaming on a balmy hot summer's evening, but should the weather play its usual tricks, and you have to resort to coming indoors, it will still taste delicious.

Curry pastes and powders vary in strength, so go carefully. The curry flavour should lurk in the background and not be so hot that the taste of mango is lost. If you use a mild garam masala powder you will need 2 tablespoons but if you have a medium or hot powder or paste reduce the amount accordingly. Choose mangoes that are ripe, but try to catch them before they get too juicy and need, as they say, to be peeled in the bath.

SERVES 6

50g/1³/₄oz butter

1 large Spanish onion, peeled and chopped

1–2 tablespoons curry paste or powder

zest and juice ½ lime

500ml/18fl oz light chicken or vegetable stock

500ml/18fl oz pressed apple juice

1 tablespoon cornflour

2 egg yolks

200ml/7fl oz crème fraîche, sour cream or double cream

2 ripe mangoes

1 tablespoon mango chutney

Melt the butter in a large pan and cook the onion until soft. Stir in the curry paste or powder and the lime zest. Cook for 1 minute before adding the stock. Stir in a few tablespoons of apple juice to the cornflour to make a smooth paste, add it and the remaining juice to the pan. Bring the soup to the boil and simmer for 10 minutes.

◆ Beat the egg yolks into the cream then slowly add a couple of ladlefuls of the soup. Pour this mixture back into the pan and stir over a gentle heat until the soup has thickened.

◆ Season the soup then leave to cool. Strain the liquid into a bowl and put the onion into a food processor or blender. Cut the mango from its stone, peel and add the flesh to the food processor or blender with the chutney. Reduce to a purée then stir it into the reserved liquid. Check the seasoning and add a squeeze of lime juice, tasting as you go.

TO FREEZE **Pour into a rigid freezer container.**

TO DEFROST **Leave for at least 15 hours in the fridge.**

TO MICROWAVE **Not suitable.**

TO EAT COLD **Stir the soup well and serve well chilled.**

CHILLED MUSSEL SOUP WITH ORANGE

I hadn't thought of this dish as freezer-friendly until a friend told me that she had made something similar for a party and frozen it and that none of her guests had guessed that it wasn't freshly cooked. I was really pleased with this version, with tomatoes, peppers and the delicious flavour of the orange pervading the whole dish.

SERVES 6

1.8kg/4lb fresh mussels

3 tablespoons olive oil

150ml/5fl oz dry white wine

2 shallots, peeled and finely chopped

2–3 cloves garlic, peeled and finely chopped

1 small red pepper, deseeded and sliced thinly

4 ripe tomatoes, peeled and roughly chopped

zest 1 and juice 2 large oranges

½ teaspoon dried chilli flakes

TO EAT COLD

small bunch flat-leaf parsley, chopped

Wash the mussels well, removing any beard and barnacles and discarding any that remain open even if tapped sharply on the side of the sink. Heat 1 tablespoon of the oil and the wine in a large pan. Add half the mussels, cover and cook over a high heat for 3-4 minutes or until all the mussels are open. Use a slotted spoon to remove the mussels to a dish and cook the remainder in the same way. Strain the cooking juices and reserve. Remove the mussels from their shells, adding any strained juices to the rest.

In a clean pan heat the remaining oil and sauté the shallots, garlic and pepper for a few minutes, then add the tomatoes, orange zest and chilli flakes. Stir, then add the reserved cooking juices and orange juice. Bring to the boil and simmer gently for a few minutes, stirring occasionally, to combine the flavours. Season to taste and leave to cool.

TO FREEZE **Put the mussels into a rigid freezer container and pour over the soup.**
TO DEFROST **Leave for 5–6 hours on the side or for at least 15 hours in the fridge.**
TO MICROWAVE **Not suitable.**
TO EAT COLD **Turn into a large dish or separate bowls and sprinkle with parsley.**
TO SERVE **Provide plenty of warm ciabatta or similar bread to mop up the juices.**

❄ CALABRESE AND GOAT'S CHEESE SOUP ⱽ

Calabrese takes up the flavour of cheese well and a light chèvre adds a subtle taste that is difficult to identify but very agreeable. If you can't find calabrese, broccoli is a good substitute.

SERVES 6

25g/1oz butter

1 medium onion, peeled and chopped

2 medium potatoes, about 350g/12oz, peeled and cubed

1.5 litres/2³/₄ pints vegetable or light chicken stock

500g/1lb 2oz calabrese, separated into florets

125g/4¹/₂oz chèvre blanc or 200g/7oz mild soft goat's cheese

In a large pan melt the butter and gently soften the onion for a few minutes. Stir in the potatoes and cook, stirring occasionally, until they have taken up most of the butter. Heat the stock, pour it in and simmer for around 5 minutes, then add the calabrese. Continue simmering for a further 15 minutes or until the onion and potato are quite tender.

◆ Drain off and reserve the liquid, and put the vegetables into a food processor or blender. Cut any rind from the cheese, chop it into pieces, and add to the vegetables. Reduce everything to a purée then return it to the liquid and season to taste.

TO FREEZE **Pour into rigid freezer containers.**

TO DEFROST **Leave on the side for several hours or overnight in the refrigerator.**

TO MICROWAVE **Follow your microwave instructions to defrost and to reheat.**

TO REHEAT **Heat gently. Do stir frequently or it may burn on the bottom.**

TO SERVE **Serve with crusty bread.**

❄ SQUASH SOUP WITH GARLIC AND THYME ⱽ

Squash or pumpkin soup is one of my real favourites and the addition of smoked garlic and thyme gives it a wonderful subtle taste. Smoked garlic can be found at many delicatessens, but you can substitute juicy cloves of ordinary garlic.

SERVES 6–8

1.3–1.5kg/3lb–3lb 5oz squash or pumpkin

50g/1³/₄oz butter

2 tablespoons oil

1 large onion, peeled and chopped

1.5 litres/2³/₄ pints light vegetable or chicken stock

2–3 cloves smoked garlic, peeled

3 sprigs thyme or 1 teaspoon dried thyme

Peel the pumpkin or squash, discard all seeds and fibre, and cut the flesh into chunks.

◆ In a large pan heat the butter and oil and sauté the onion until it has softened. Add the squash, cover the pan, and cook gently for 10 minutes. Pour in the stock, bring to the boil and simmer for 20 minutes. Halve the garlic cloves, discard any green centre shoots, then roughly chop the rest and add to the soup with the thyme leaves stripped from the stems. Simmer for a further 10 minutes or until the squash is very soft. Drain off and reserve the liquid and purée the vegetables in a food processor or blender. Stir the purée back into the liquid and season lightly.

TO FREEZE **Turn into rigid freezer containers.**

TO DEFROST **Leave on the side for 5–6 hours or overnight in the fridge.**

TO MICROWAVE **Follow your microwave instructions for defrosting and reheating.**

TO REHEAT **Dilute the defrosted soup with stock or water to achieve a good consistency. Check the seasoning then heat, stirring constantly, until very hot.**

TO SERVE **Serve in warm bowls with some croûtons and toasted pumpkin seeds.**

SQUASH SOUP WITH GARLIC AND THYME

❄ AUBERGINE AND MELTED MOZZARELLA ROLLS WITH HOT TOMATO VINAIGRETTE ⱽ

These rolls consist of aubergine slices wrapped round a piece of mozzarella cheese and bathed in tomato vinaigrette, which adds the most wonderful flavour. I have tried eating them cold but they are much nicer served hot with the cheese all melted and gooey.

To salt or not always seems to be the question with aubergines. For this recipe I prefer to salt them as it draws out some of the moisture and they seem to need less oil when they are fried.

SERVES 6
3 aubergines, trimmed
oil for frying
2 mozzarellas
Tomato Vinaigrette (opposite)

Hold an aubergine upright on your chopping board and shave off and discard an outside slice. Cut 6 slices, discarding the other outside slice with the skin. Repeat with the other aubergines then lay the slices on the draining board. Sprinkle with salt, leave for about $1/2$ hour then turn them over and salt the other side. Leave for a further 20 minutes. Rinse the slices in a bowl of cold water. Gently pat dry on clean tea towels.

◆ Cook the slices either on a ridged grill pan or fry them on both sides in some cooking oil. The cooked slices need to be soft throughout and a streaked golden brown colour. Sandwich the cooked slices between layers of kitchen paper and leave to cool.

◆ Cut each mozzarella into 9 even chunks. I find the easiest way is to cut them like a cake. Put a chunk of cheese onto an aubergine slice and roll it up. Repeat with the other slices and lay them neatly into a freezer- and ovenproof gratin dish. Whisk the vinaigrette together then generously spoon some over the rolls; you will probably use just over half of the amount in the recipe. The remainder can be frozen separately.

TO FREEZE **Cover the dish with foil. Freeze the remaining vinaigrette separately.**
TO DEFROST **Leave on the side for 6–7 hours or for at least 15 hours in the fridge.**
TO MICROWAVE **Not suitable.**
TO REHEAT **Heat the oven to 200°C/400°F/gas 6, put in the defrosted dish and cook for 20 minutes or until the cheese has just melted. Warm the reserved Tomato Vinaigrette either in a pan or in the microwave.**
TO SERVE **Serve immediately on hot plates with the extra sauce spooned over the rolls and some crusty bread.**

❄ TOMATO VINAIGRETTE ᵛ

This vinaigrette sauce, hot or cold, gives a great lift to many dishes. Try it cold with the Gruyère and Ricotta Mousses (page 32) and the Salmon and Spinach Terrine (page 37). It is also delicious, with garlic added, drizzled over salade niçoise. The sauce benefits from using really sweet-flavoured ripe fruit; otherwise it may need a little sugar adding.

MAKES ABOUT 300ml/10fl oz
400g/14oz ripe tomatoes
3 tablespoons raspberry vinegar
150ml/5fl oz fruity olive oil

Put the tomatoes into a food processor or blender and reduce to a purée. Strain the purée through a sieve into a saucepan, pushing as much of the tomato flesh through as you can. Bring slowly to the boil then simmer, stirring occasionally, until the purée has been reduced by half to two-thirds. Take from the heat and leave until cold.

◆ To make the sauce whisk together the vinegar, oil, 5-6 tablespoons of the tomato purée and season to taste.

TO FREEZE **Freeze in batches to use as required. Pour into freezer-proof jars or containers.**
TO DEFROST **Leave on the side for 3 hours or in the fridge for 6 hours.**
TO MICROWAVE **Not suitable.**
TO FINISH **Whisk thoroughly before use.**

❄ CAPONATA DI MELANZANE ᵛ

Caponata is the Sicilian version of the better-known ratatouille. The mixture of sautéed aubergines and celery which is then added to a sweet-sour tomato sauce gives this dish a pleasant astringency.

SERVES 6
750g/1lb 10oz aubergines
125ml/4fl oz olive oil
1 large Spanish onion, peeled and coarsely chopped
inside sticks of a head of celery, chopped
400g/14oz can tomatoes
1 tablespoon dark brown sugar
50ml/2 fl oz red or white wine vinegar
75g/2³⁄₄oz large green olives, stoned and quartered
50g/1³⁄₄oz capers

TO FINISH
small bunch basil leaves
handful pinenuts, toasted

Top and tail the aubergines, cut them into 2cm/³⁄₄in dice then turn them into a colander and sprinkle with a spoonful of salt. Put a weight on the top and leave them to drain for 1 hour.

◆ Quickly rinse the aubergine under a cold tap then dry on kitchen paper. In a large pan heat the oil and fry the dice, turning them constantly, until they start to brown. Add the onion and, when soft, the celery. Cook gently until tender. Drain the juice from the tomatoes and add them to the pan together with the sugar, vinegar, olives and capers. Season to taste, then cook, stirring frequently, for 15 minutes.

TO FREEZE **Turn into a freezer- and ovenproof dish, covered with foil.**
TO DEFROST **Leave on the side for 7–8 hours or in the fridge for 16–18 hours.**
TO MICROWAVE **Not suitable.**
TO REHEAT **Heat in the oven at 160°C/325°F/gas 3 for 20–25 minutes or until warm.**
TO FINISH **Scatter with torn basil leaves and toasted pinenuts.**
TO SERVE **Serve with lots of warm Italian-style bread drizzled with olive oil.**

❄ ROASTED MEDITERRANEAN VEGETABLES ⱽ

A variety of summer vegetables chopped up and roasted together makes a delicious hot or cold starter and I give instructions for serving it both ways. I was thrilled to discover that the final dish, eaten either hot or cold, is just as good after a week or two in the freezer. The vegetables are also wonderful used more substantially as a filling for a lasagne and I give the recipe on page 104.

If by happy chance you should find fresh baby artichokes, snap them up, but canned ones are a good substitute. Likewise, if you should find baby plum tomatoes, snap those up too.

SERVES 6

1 large aubergine

2 courgettes

1 red onion

1 large red pepper or 1 small red and 1 small yellow pepper

400g/14oz ripe plum tomatoes

150ml/5fl oz olive oil

6 artichoke hearts, fresh or canned

3 cloves garlic

handful basil leaves

100g/3½oz black olives

2 tablespoons capers, rinsed

TO REHEAT OR EAT COLD

a little olive oil

handful basil leaves (optional)

Set the oven to heat to its maximum while you prepare the vegetables. Dice the aubergine and courgettes into bite-sized pieces, peel and roughly chop the onion. Deseed the pepper and cut the flesh into short strips. Skin the tomatoes and, depending on size, leave them whole or cut into halves or quarters.

◆ Put everything into a roasting tin, sprinkle on some salt and pepper, drizzle over the oil and turn the vegetables to make sure they are all covered with oil. Put the tin in the hot oven for 15 minutes then add the artichoke hearts, garlic and roughly torn basil leaves. Give everything a good stir and return the pan to the oven. If you plan to reheat the vegetables to eat hot, leave for a further 5 minutes. If you plan to eat them cold, leave to cook for a further 20 minutes or until they are browning round the edges. Take from the oven and stir in the olives and capers.

TO FREEZE **Turn into a rigid freezer container.**

TO DEFROST **Leave for 7–8 hours on the side or for 15–18 hours in the fridge.**

TO MICROWAVE **Not suitable.**

TO REHEAT **Preheat the oven to 220°C/425°F/gas7. Return everything to a roasting tin and check the seasoning. Roast for a further 20–25 minutes, by which time everything will be sizzling and browning at the edges.**

TO EAT COLD **Stir the defrosted vegetables and spoon into a serving dish. Drizzle on a little more olive oil and sprinkle with some fresh basil, if liked.**

TO SERVE **Serve immediately, hot or cold, with plenty of warm crusty bread and extra olive oil for drizzling.**

❄ MIDDLE EASTERN SALAD WITH CURRIED PARSNIP CUBES ⓥ

This is a fusion of Middle Eastern flavours with Jane Grigson's well-known combination of parsnips and curry spices. The result makes a first course.

You can use either Spanish onions or the American 'no tears' variety that is now widely available. Curry powder or pastes come in different strengths and for this recipe add just enough to tickle the palate nicely but not so much that your eyes start to water.

SERVES 6

2 large onions, peeled and chopped

50g/1³⁄₄oz butter

4 tablespoons oil

1–2 teaspoons curry paste or powder

3 cloves garlic, peeled and chopped

75g/2³⁄₄oz raisins

650g/1lb 7oz parsnips, trimmed and peeled

50g/1³⁄₄oz pinenuts

TO FINISH

bunch coriander

150ml/5fl oz Greek yoghurt

Gently sauté the onions in a pan with the butter and 1 tablespoon of the oil until soft. Stir in the curry paste or powder, then add the garlic and raisins and leave to stew gently for 5-10 minutes.

◆ Meanwhile, cut the parsnips into bite-sized cubes. In a frying pan or wok heat the remaining oil and fry the parsnips until they are cooked and golden brown. Remove and drain on kitchen paper. Put the pinenuts into the pan, quickly brown, then remove to a plate.

◆ Take the onion mixture from the heat, season to taste then stir in the parsnips and pinenuts.

TO FREEZE **Pack in a plastic container.**
TO DEFROST **Leave on the side for 6–7 hours or in the fridge overnight for at least 15 hours.**
TO MICROWAVE **Not suitable.**
TO FINISH **Chop the coriander and stir into the yoghurt and hand it round the table with the defrosted salad.**

❄ HOT BROAD BEAN MOUSSE WITH RICH MUSHROOM SAUCE ⱽ

Broad beans freeze very well and I make this bright green mousse using a pack of frozen ones. If using fresh ones, you will probably need 3 times the weight of unshelled beans.

SERVES 6

600g/1lb 5oz frozen broad beans

4 eggs

300ml/10fl oz single cream

TO FINISH

Rich Mushroom Sauce (below)

Tip the frozen beans into a pan of boiling salted water, bring it back to the boil and simmer for 3 minutes. Drain and immediately put the beans under a running cold tap to set the colour. Now pop them from their skins by nicking the end of each bean and squeezing.

◆ Put the beans into a food processor or blender and reduce to a purée. Add the eggs, cream and seasonings and pulse the machine a few times which should be enough to mix them in. Turn the mixture into a well-greased ring mould.

TO FREEZE **Cover with foil or a double layer of cling film.**

TO DEFROST **Defrost overnight or for at least 15 hours in the fridge. Do not let it warm up to room temperature.**

TO MICROWAVE **Not suitable.**

TO COOK **Preheat the oven to 200°C/400°F/gas 5. Put the defrosted mould, covered with greased foil, into a bain-marie and cook for 50 minutes.**

TO FINISH **Run a knife round the inside of the mould then turn it out onto a platter. Fill the centre with the Rich Mushroom Sauce and serve any extra separately.**

❄ RICH MUSHROOM SAUCE ⱽ

I make this sauce with open mushrooms which I think go best with ceps. It, too, can be frozen.

SERVES 6

10g/¼oz dried cep mushrooms

100g/3½oz small open mushrooms

50g/1¾oz butter

1 shallot, peeled and chopped

150ml/5fl oz single cream

Soak the dried cep in 300ml/10fl oz water for at least ½ hour. Remove the mushrooms and roughly chop. Strain the liquid through a very fine sieve or piece of muslin to remove any grains of sand.

◆ Peel the flat mushrooms, discard the stalks, and cut them in thin strips then cut the strips into short lengths.

◆ Melt the butter, soften the shallot then add all the mushrooms and a good pinch of salt. Cook, stirring until soft, then pour in the soaking liquid and simmer until it has reduced by two-thirds. Stir in the cream, simmer for 2-3 minutes and adjust the seasoning. Take from the heat and leave to cool.

TO FREEZE **Pour into a rigid freezer container.**

TO DEFROST **Leave on the side for 3–4 hours or in the fridge for at least 5–6 hours.**

TO MICROWAVE **Follow your microwave instructions for defrosting and reheating.**

TO REHEAT **Pour the sauce into a pan, put on the hob and heat, stirring frequently, until hot.**

❄ CHEESE SOUFFLES ᵛ

For a long time I have known that you can make up a soufflé and hold it in the fridge for several hours before baking it, and when starting on this book I suddenly thought of going one stage further and freezing it. Eureka! It worked.

This is the basic and ever useful cheese soufflé which can be served for a first course, a supper main course or for a savoury. I find that individual-sized soufflés freeze better - either use ramekins or for something more substantial small soufflé dishes. Fill the dishes up to three-quarters full. This recipe makes enough to fill 8 ramekins or 5-6 soufflé dishes.

Whatever cheese you use it needs to be a hard one: a mixture of cheddar and gruyère is good, or try parmesan and cheddar, double gloucester and cheddar or just cheddar.

SERVES 5–8

40g/1¹/₂oz butter plus extra for greasing

350ml/12fl oz milk

1 small bay leaf

few parsley stalks

4–5 peppercorns, lightly crushed

40g/1¹/₂oz plain flour

4 egg yolks

100g/3¹/₂oz cheese, grated

1 teaspoon Dijon mustard

5 egg whites

Melt the extra butter and grease the insides of the the soufflé or ramekin dishes well (I use a pastry brush).

◆ First you need to make a bechamel sauce so put the milk, bay leaf, parsley stalks and peppercorns into a pan and bring slowly to the boil. Take from the heat and leave to cool slightly, stirring occasionally to prevent a skin forming.

◆ In another pan melt the butter, stir in the flour and cook gently, stirring all the while, for 2-3 minutes before straining in the milk. Bring to the boil, stirring constantly to achieve a thick smooth bechamel sauce. Let it bubble for 2-3 minutes before removing from the heat. Leave to cool for 5 minutes then add, one by one, the egg yolks, stirring well to incorporate each one before adding the next. Season well then stir in the mustard and the cheese.

◆ Whisk the egg whites until stiff and 'relax' the cheese mixture by stirring in a spoonful of egg white. Gently fold in the rest with a large metal spoon. Spoon the mixture in dollops into the centre of the prepared dishes so that you have clean sides and a rounded top to the soufflés.

TO FREEZE **Cover with foil or a double layer of cling film.**

TO DEFROST **They are best cooked from frozen.**

TO MICROWAVE **Not suitable.**

TO COOK **Preheat the oven to 200°C/400°F/gas 6 and cook the soufflés, uncovered, for 35–40 minutes for large ones and 25–30 for ramekins or until they are risen and golden brown on the top. Serve immediately.**

❄ CALABRESE SOUFFLES WITH TAPENADE ⱽ

These soufflés have a lovely colour and an elusive taste. Served with croûtons and tapenade they make a very elegant first course. Tapenade can be bought in jars but it is easy to make your own. It keeps in a screwtop jar in the fridge for a week; otherwise put in the freezer with the soufflés.

SERVES 6–10 DEPENDING ON THE SIZE OF THE DISHES

40g/1½oz butter plus extra for greasing

350ml/12fl oz milk

1 small bay leaf

few parsley stalks

4–5 peppercorns, lightly crushed

250g/9oz calabrese or broccoli, trimmed

40g/1½oz plain flour

4 egg yolks

25g/1oz parmesan, grated

scraping nutmeg

5 egg whites

FOR THE TAPENADE

150g/5½oz plump black olives, stoned

1 teaspoon capers, washed

3 anchovy fillets

1 clove garlic, peeled

juice ½ lemon

1 teaspoon fresh thyme, chopped

75ml/2½fl oz olive oil

TO FINISH

fresh bread, thinly sliced

Melt the extra butter and grease the insides of the soufflé or ramekin dishes well.

◆ Put the milk, bay leaf, parsley stalks and peppercorns into a pan and bring slowly to the boil. Take from the heat and leave to cool, stirring occasionally to prevent a skin forming.

◆ Bring a pan of salted water to the boil, add the calabrese and cook until tender. Drain and leave to steam and dry off for 2 minutes then reduce to a purée in a food processor or blender.

◆ Melt the butter, stir in the flour and cook for 1 minute before straining in the milk. Whisk to produce a smooth sauce, then bring to the boil and let it bubble, still stirring, for 2 minutes. Remove the pan from the heat, add the calabrese and, one by one, stir in the egg yolks. Finally stir in the cheese and season to taste with salt, pepper and a scraping of nutmeg.

◆ Whisk the egg whites until stiff and gently fold the soufflé mixture into them. Spoon into the prepared dishes as for the Cheese Soufflés on page 25.

◆ To make the tapenade, whizz all the ingredients except the oil to a purée in a food processor or blender, then, with the machine still running, slowly add the oil through the feed tube.

TO FREEZE **Cover each dish with foil or a double layer of cling film. Freeze tapenade in a separate container.**

TO DEFROST **Best cooked from frozen.**

TO MICROWAVE **Not suitable.**

TO COOK **Heat the oven to 200°C/400°F/gas 6 and cook the uncovered soufflés for 25–30 minutes for small ones and 35–45 minutes for larger ones or until they have risen and have browned on top.**

TO FINISH **Toast the bread and spread each piece with tapenade. Serve with soufflés as soon as they are ready.**

❄ SOUFFLES HELVETICA ⱽ

Another way of preparing and freezing soufflés in which they are baked twice. The mixture for Soufflés Helvetica, or Swiss soufflés, is slightly thicker and denser than the standard cheese one. They are cooked in individual ramekins, left to cool then frozen. After defrosting they are covered with cream flavoured with garlic, then heated briefly in a very hot oven from which they emerge, delicious, browned and bubbling. Garlic adds a lovely dimension to the dish but you could omit it, in which case I suggest you stir some cheese into the cream and sprinkle a little more over the top just before putting the soufflés into the oven.

SERVES 6

50g/1¾oz butter plus extra for
   greasing
50g/1¾oz flour
300ml/10fl oz milk
1 bay leaf
pinch nutmeg
175g/6oz gruyère, grated
5 eggs, separated

TO COOK
425ml/15fl oz single cream
2 cloves garlic, peeled and
   quartered
40g/1½oz butter
2 teaspoons flour

Generously butter 6 ramekins. Heat the oven to 190°C/375°F/gas 5 and put in a roasting tin half full of hot water.

◆ Melt the butter, stir in the flour and cook gently for 1-2 minutes, then stir in the milk, add the bay leaf and bring to the boil. Simmer, stirring, for a further 1-2 minutes, before taking the pan from the heat, removing the bay leaf, and seasoning the sauce with salt, pepper and a little nutmeg. Let it cool a little, stir in the cheese, then, one by one, the egg yolks.

◆ Whisk the egg whites until stiff and stir a large spoonful into the cheese mixture to slacken it. Fold in the remainder and then spoon the mixture into the prepared ramekins. Put the ramekins into the hot bain-marie and cook for 25-30 minutes or until the soufflés are risen and quite firm.

◆ Leave the soufflés to cool, and don't worry - they will shrink.

TO FREEZE Before freezing loosen each soufflé by running a knife round each one and turning them over so that they drop out onto your hand. Return the soufflés to the ramekins and cover with foil or a double layer of cling film.

TO DEFROST After a couple of hours in the fridge they should be fairly easy to turn out of the ramekins. Place in a buttered shallow ovenproof dish, not too big, so that they fit snugly. Leave in the fridge for 3–4 hours to finish defrosting.

TO MICROWAVE Not suitable.

TO COOK Pour the cream into a saucepan and add the garlic cloves. Bring it to boiling point, remove it from the heat and leave to infuse for ½ hour. Mix the butter and flour together to make a beurre manié. Heat the oven to 220°C/425°F/gas 7. Remove and discard the garlic, season the cream, put it back on the heat and stir in the beurre manié. Bring to the boil and stir until you have a smooth sauce. Take the pan from the heat, pour the cream over the soufflés and immediately put them in the hot oven and cook for 12–15 minutes. Serve immediately.

❄ ARTICHOKE HEART SOUFFLES ⱽ

A good and unusual variation on the basic soufflé is to flavour it with mashed artichoke hearts. Any hearts remaining in the tin can be cut into 2 or 3 and put into the dishes and then covered with the soufflé mixture.

MAKES 5–8

40g/1½oz butter plus extra for greasing

40g/1½oz flour

350ml/12fl oz milk

5 artichoke hearts, tinned

4 egg yolks

2 tablespoons parmesan, grated

5 egg whites

Melt the extra butter and grease the insides of small soufflé dishes or ramekins well.

◆ Make a bechamel sauce with the butter, flour and milk following the instructions in the recipe for Cheese Soufflés on page 25.

◆ Put the artichoke bottoms into a food processor or blender with a couple of spoonfuls of sauce and reduce to a purée. Stir the purée into the remaining sauce. Let it cool slightly then stir in the egg yolks, cheese and season. Fold in the stiffly beaten egg whites and spoon into the soufflé dishes or ramekins.

TO FREEZE, TO DEFROST AND TO COOK **Follow the instructions for the Cheese Soufflés on page 25.**

❄ CALABRESE AND DOLCELATTE FILO PURSES ⱽ

These little filo purses are filled with a delicious mixture of flavours and can be served, as suggested here, as a first course or you could double the quantities for a light lunch dish. I find that broccoli works just as well as calabrese.

SERVES 6

200–250g/7–9oz head of calabrese, cut into small florets

150ml/5fl oz sour cream

1 teaspoon cornflour

2 tablespoons milk

100g/3½oz dolcelatte

6 sheets filo pastry

First of all make the filling. Discard the stalks of the calabrese and plunge the florets into a pan of boiling salted water and cook for 4-5 minutes or until tender. Drain and rinse under a cold tap to retain the colour.

◆ Pour the sour cream into a small pan and put to warm on the hob. Slake the cornflour in the milk, stir it into the sour cream and bring it all to the boil. Stir until it has thickened then crumble in the dolcelatte and let it melt. Take the pan from the heat. Season to taste with a little salt if needed and a good grinding of pepper.

TO FREEZE, TO DEFROST AND TO COOK **Follow the instructions for Asparagus and Filo Purses (opposite).** TO SERVE **Serve hot, garnished with some dressed green leaves sprinkled with a few chopped toasted walnuts.**

❄ ASPARAGUS AND FILO PURSES ᵛ

Imported asparagus is now available all year round and these little filo purses make as good and welcome a first course in spring or autumn as they do during the season for homegrown asparagus. I think it would be a waste to use best-quality English asparagus but you may be able to find offcuts or sprue.

SERVES 6

250g/9oz asparagus

2 eggs and 1 egg yolk

25g/1oz fresh breadcrumbs

2 tablespoons parmesan, freshly grated

3 tablespoons cream

40g/1½oz butter

6 sheets filo pastry, defrosted

Cook the asparagus until tender then refresh it by plunging it immediately into a bowl of cold water. Drain and lay on a tea towel to dry. Cut off and keep the tips and discard any woody base to the stalks. Roughly chop the stalks, put them in a food processor or blender together with the eggs, egg yolk, breadcrumbs, parmesan and cream, and reduce everything to a purée. Turn the purée into a bowl, season to taste, and stir in the tips, cut in half if they are long ones. Put the mixture to cool in the fridge for ½ hour.

◆ Melt the butter. Lay a piece of filo pastry on your work surface, cut it in half and then cut each half into three. Take a piece and, using a pastry brush, lightly spread both sides with butter. Put it into a deep muffin tin or a ramekin, with a corner standing up above the sides but be careful not to press it in too hard or the pastry will tear. Put in a further four pieces of pastry all at an angle to each other. Spoon in some of the asparagus mixture and then turn over the ends of the pastry and finally cover the top with the final piece of pastry which has been buttered and then lightly crumpled up. Repeat for the remaining 5 ramekins.

TO FREEZE **If possible freeze the purses in their tins or ramekins, otherwise remove them to a rigid freezer container.**

TO DEFROST **Leave on the side for 5–6 hours, in the fridge overnight or you can cook them before they are fully defrosted.**

TO MICROWAVE **Not suitable.**

TO COOK **Put a baking tray into the oven and heat it to 190°C/375°F/gas 5. Leave the purses in the muffin tin or put them onto the hot baking tray and bake for 20 minutes or until the pastry is crisp and golden.**

TO SERVE **Serve hot or warm, garnished with a little fresh asparagus or some lightly dressed salad leaves.**

❄ ASPARAGUS-FILLED PANCAKES ⱽ

Pancakes are a well-known freezer standby and justifiably so, as they can be time-consuming to make, and they really do freeze perfectly. They can be frozen, unfilled, interleaved with greaseproof paper, or they can be filled and rolled before freezing. This basic recipe allows 2 pancakes per person which makes a fairly substantial first course or light lunch, but you can always alter the amount. The asparagus filling is one of my favourites, and there is no need to use best-quality seasonal asparagus. I use imported asparagus tips which are cheaper and available throughout the year.

SERVES 6

FOR THE PANCAKES

150g/5^1/$_2$oz flour

2 eggs

1 tablespoon sunflower oil

400ml/14fl oz milk

butter for greasing

FOR THE FILLING

200g/7oz asparagus tips

85g/3oz butter

50g/1^3/$_4$oz flour

300ml/10fl oz milk

bunch chives, snipped

bunch basil, chopped

50g/1^3/$_4$oz parmesan, grated

Start by making the batter. Put the flour, eggs, oil and seasoning into a food processor or blender. Start the machine and then slowly pour in the milk through the feed tube. When the mixture is a smooth consistency pour into a jug and refrigerate for about an hour before making the pancakes.

◆ Heat an 18cm/7in pan and spread a little butter over the base. Pour a little batter into the hot pan and shake the pan to spread it out. Cook the pancake for 1-2 minutes or until the bottom has browned and then flip to cook the other side. Put the pancake onto a plate and cover with greaseproof paper. Repeat to use all the batter: it makes around 15-18 pancakes and you need 12 for this recipe but the others can be frozen as they are and used another time.

◆ Cook the asparagus by laying the tips flat in a wide sauté pan, and covering them with boiling water and some salt. Simmer for 5 minutes or until tender, then drain, reserving the cooking liquid.

◆ Melt 50g/1^3/$_4$oz of the butter, stir in the flour and slowly add the milk and 300ml/10fl oz of the reserved liquid. Bring to the boil and stir until you have a smooth sauce. Let it bubble gently, stirring from time to time, for 3-4 minutes then take from the heat and add the herbs and the parmesan.

◆ Melt two-thirds of the remaining butter and use a pastry brush to grease a gratin or shallow freezer- and ovenproof dish.

◆ Take a pancake, spread a good spoonful of the sauce up the centre, put 3-4 (depending on the number you have) asparagus spears on top, roll up the pancake and put it into the dish. Repeat with 11 more pancakes. Melt the remaining butter and brush it over the top and ends of the pancakes.

▼ Between making each pancake I find it easiest to scrunch up a wad of kitchen paper and use it to spread a film of butter onto the pan.

TO FREEZE **Cover with foil or a double layer of cling film.**

TO DEFROST **Leave for 5–6 hours on the side or overnight in the fridge.**

TO MICROWAVE **Follow your microwave instructions for defrosting and reheating.**

TO REHEAT **Cover the dish with foil and heat at 180°C/350°F/gas 4 for 30–35 minutes. You can reheat it from frozen or from partially frozen but it will take considerably longer.**

❄ CHIVE PANCAKES WITH DOUBLE CHEESE AND ROASTED TOMATO FILLING ⱽ

Herby pancakes filled with a mixture of cream cheese and parmesan jazzed up with roast tomatoes and pinenuts add up to something really good.

SERVES 6

FOR THE PANCAKES

75g/2³/₄oz flour

1 egg

200ml/7fl oz milk

1 tablespoon sunflower oil

bunch chives, snipped

FOR THE FILLING

8–12 ripe tomatoes, depending on size

a little olive oil

200g/7oz soft cream cheese

40g/1¹/₂oz parmesan, grated

4–5 spring onions, chopped

bunch basil, chopped

75g/2³/₄oz pinenuts

cayenne (optional)

20g/³/₄oz butter

Make the batter according to the recipe on page 30. When the mixture is smooth pour it into a jug, stir in the chives and refrigerate for about an hour before cooking the pancakes.

◆ Meanwhile, halve the tomatoes, place in a roasting tray or shallow gratin dish and drizzle a little olive oil over each one. Roast at 190°C/375°F/gas 5 for ³/₄ hour.

◆ Cook the pancakes using a small 14cm/5¹/₂in pan following the method in the previous recipe. You need 12 for this recipe but the others can be frozen as they are and used another time.

◆ Scrape out the inside of the tomatoes and put the flesh and the two cheeses into a food processor or blender. Blend everything together then add the spring onions and the basil and blend them in.

◆ Toast the pinenuts in a small frying pan, tossing them over a medium heat to brown all over. Turn the cheese and tomato mixture into a bowl, stir in the pinenuts and season with salt, pepper and, if liked, a little cayenne.

◆ Divide the mixture between the pancakes, roll them up and put into a gratin or shallow freezer- and ovenproof dish. Melt the butter and brush it over the pancakes.

TO FREEZE **Cover with foil or a double layer of cling film.**

TO DEFROST **Leave for 5–6 hours on the side or overnight in the fridge.**

TO MICROWAVE **Follow your microwave instructions for defrosting and reheating.**

TO REHEAT **Cover the dish with foil and heat at 180°C/350°F/gas 4 for 30–35 minutes. It may be reheated from frozen or partially frozen but it will take considerably longer.**

GRUYERE AND RICOTTA MOUSSES WITH TOMATO VINAIGRETTE (v)

These fresh-tasting little mousses make a lovely light first course or they could be served, instead of cheese, at the end of the meal. Serve with a vinaigrette dressing with lots of herbs chopped into it or, best of all, with Tomato Vinaigrette (page 21) spooned into each ramekin. The amount here is enough to fill 8 ramekins but if you want to be generous you can fill 6 ramekins almost to the top.

SERVES 6–8

75g/2³/₄oz gruyère

250g/9oz ricotta

150ml/5fl oz (150g/5¹/₂oz) plain yoghurt

2 leaves gelatine

juice ¹/₂ lemon

tabasco or cayenne

2 egg whites

TO FINISH

200ml/7fl oz Tomato Vinaigrette (page 21)

6–8 basil leaves

OR

200ml/7fl oz vinaigrette

1 tablespoon parsley, chopped

1 tablespoon chives, snipped

Finely grate the gruyère then mix well with the ricotta and yoghurt – ideally in a food processor.

◆ Soak the gelatine in cold water for 5 minutes. In a small bowl heat the lemon juice together with 1 tablespoon water. (Easily done in the microwave.) Stir the soaked gelatine into the hot lemon juice and when it has melted stir, or process, it into the cheese mixture. Season well, and add a shake or two of tabasco or a pinch of cayenne. Whisk the egg whites until stiff and fold them into the mixture.

◆ Spoon into 6 or 8 ramekins.

TO FREEZE **Cover the ramekins with foil or a double layer of cling film.**

TO DEFROST **Take from the freezer and leave in the fridge for 4–5 hours or on the side for 2–3 hours.**

TO MICROWAVE **Not suitable.**

TO FINISH **Into each ramekin pour some vinaigrette sauce with chopped parsley and chives stirred into it, or some Tomato Vinaigrette, and garnish with a basil leaf.**

❄ BASIL AND TOMATO RING ⱽ

Like many people I am passionate about basil and this recipe includes a good handful of it. A jellied tomato ring is one of the most useful and versatile of dishes and can be filled with almost anything that takes your fancy. The filling I give below always goes down a treat. For an easy vegetarian alternative you could leave out the prawns and add a handful of shredded celeriac or chopped watercress.

SERVES 6–8

6 sheets gelatine

2 x 400g/14oz cans tomatoes

1 tablespoon demerara sugar

zest ½ lime or lemon

1 tablespoon sherry

3–5 spring onions, finely chopped

large bunch basil, chopped

TO FINISH

3 tablespoons mayonnaise

3 tablespoons crème fraîche

75g/2¾oz button mushrooms

1 avocado

225g/8oz prawns, peeled

Soak the gelatine leaves in a bowl of cold water. Turn the tomatoes into a food processor or blender, reduce to a smooth purée then sieve to eliminate any pips. Put about 300ml/10fl oz of the purée into a pan with the sugar and citrus zest and heat gently. When it is hot, but not boiling, stir in the drained gelatine. Add the mixture to the rest of the purée then stir in the sherry, spring onions and basil and season well.

◆ Turn into a wet 850ml/1½ pint ring mould. You can pour any left over into ramekins to make one or two little individual jellies.

TO FREEZE **Cover with foil or a double layer of cling film.**

TO DEFROST **Leave in the fridge for 5–6 hours.**

TO MICROWAVE **Not suitable.**

TO FINISH **Mix the mayonnaise and the crème fraîche together. Cut the stalks from the mushrooms and peel and slice them. Dice the avocado flesh and mix it together with the mushrooms and the prawns into the mayonnaise mixture and season to taste. Turn the tomato ring out onto a large plate and fill the centre with the prawn mixture.**

❄ MUSSELS STUFFED WITH ALMONDS

This recipe has its origins in southern Spain where mussels are plentiful around the coast, and inland almonds grow freely in orchards.

The prepared mussels are cooked from frozen so it is a good dish to serve when you are very short of time. Provided you don't have to discard too many, a generous kilo of mussels will give you around 60 which is just about right for a first course for 6 people. Packets of ground almonds can be rather dry and tasteless so I use whole, peeled almonds and grind them myself in a food processor.

SERVES 6

1–1.5kg/2lb 4oz–3lb 5oz large
   mussels

100ml/3^1/$_2$fl oz dry white wine or
   water

150g/5^1/$_2$oz butter

3 shallots, peeled and finely
   chopped

1 clove garlic, peeled and finely
   chopped

large bunch parsley, chopped

150g/5^1/$_2$oz ground almonds

juice 1 lemon

In a large bowl of cold water pick over and scrub the mussels, discarding any broken ones or those that remain open even if given a sharp tap. Wash them thoroughly in two or three changes of water.

◆ Heat the wine or water in a large pan, add the mussels, cover the pan and cook over a high heat, shaking the pan from time to time, for 3-4 minutes or until all the mussels have opened. Immediately remove the pan from the heat and turn the mussels into a colander to drain and cool quickly.

◆ In a frying or sauté pan melt the butter, add the shallots and garlic and cook gently until very soft, but do not let them brown. Mix together with the parsley, ground almonds and lemon juice and season to taste.

◆ Break off and throw out the lid of each cooled mussel. Use a knife to prise off any mussels still attached to the shell, then cover each one with a teaspoonful of the stuffing. Put them onto a baking tray, or something similar that will fit into your freezer.

TO FREEZE **Put the tray into the freezer and leave for around 2 hours or until well frozen. Decant the mussels into plastic bags, seal well and return to the freezer.**
TO DEFROST **Cook from frozen.**
TO MICROWAVE **Not suitable.**
TO COOK **Heat the oven to 220°C/425°F/gas 7. Return the mussels to a baking tray and put into the oven for 5 minutes. Take care not to overcook the mussels or they will go tough: remove from the oven the moment the stuffing starts to bubble.**
TO SERVE **Serve immediately with crusty bread on a bed of red chicory leaves.**

❄ SALMON MOUSSELINES WITH BEURRE BLANC SAUCE

Mousselines are often regarded as the exclusive province of the professional, but use a food processor and follow the rule of keeping everything ice cold and they are easy. Use any firm fish or shellfish; lobster is out of this world but you would need to sieve it before adding the cream. I like salmon as the flavour always comes through.

SERVES 6–8

250g/9oz salmon fillet, skinned (300g/10¹⁄₂oz before skinning)

pinch cayenne

2 scant teaspoons salt

1 whole egg and 1 egg white

350ml/12fl oz double cream

butter for greasing

TO FINISH

Beurre Blanc Sauce (below)

2 ripe tomatoes, diced

Make sure that the fish, eggs and cream are very cold, having been in the fridge for at least 2 hours. Cut the fish into chunks and whizz it in the food processor for 2 minutes, scrape it down, add the cayenne and salt and whizz for another minute. With the machine running add the egg and egg white through the feed tube. When they have amalgamated stop the machine, scrape the mix down and switch on again briefly. Put the food processor bowl into the fridge and leave for at least 1 hour.

◆ Re-fit the bowl and, with the motor running, pour the cream in through the lid in a steady stream. Then stop the machine, scrape it down again and then pulse a few times to mix everything.

◆ Spoon into 6-8 well-greased ramekins and freeze.

TO FREEZE **Cover each mould with foil or a double layer of cling film.**

TO DEFROST **Leave in the fridge for 5–6 hours or cook from frozen.**

TO MICROWAVE **Not suitable.**

TO COOK **Put a roasting tin into the oven and heat it to 180°C/350°F/gas 4. Put the moulds into the hot tin and pour in enough boiling water to come halfway up them. Cook defrosted ones for 25–30 minutes and frozen ones for 40 minutes or until spongy.**

TO FINISH **Pour the Beurre Blanc Sauce onto 6 or 8 warm plates. Take the mousselines from the oven and carefully turn each one into the centre of a plate. Decorate with the diced tomatoes and serve immediately.**

❄ BEURRE BLANC SAUCE

SERVES 6–8

2 shallots, peeled and finely chopped

4 tablespoons dry white wine

4 tablespoons white wine vinegar

1 tablespoon double cream

250g/9oz very cold unsalted butter, cubed

Put the shallots, wine and vinegar into a pan and boil to reduce the liquid to 3-4 tablespoons. Stir in the cream and boil again to reduce by half. Then over a low heat whisk in the butter, cube by cube. The sauce won't emulsify unless there is enough heat to melt the butter properly but if you go too far and it looks like overheating and separating, cool it quickly by plunging the bottom of the pan into a basin of cold water.

◆ When all the butter has been incorporated strain the sauce and season it to taste.

TO FREEZE **Not suitable.**

❄ SALMON AND SPINACH TERRINE

A simple terrine consisting of a spinach and salmon mousseline layered with slices of salmon. It is good, especially if you have a strong-flavoured meal to follow, with a dab of mayonnaise, but serve it with the Tomato Vinaigrette and it immediately becomes a different and unusual dish.

SERVES 6–8

200g/7oz fresh spinach

400g/14oz skinned and boned salmon, chilled

2 eggs

150ml/5fl oz whipping cream, chilled

nutmeg

TO FINISH

Tomato Vinaigrette (page 21) or mayonnaise

Grease a loaf tin and line with greaseproof or silicone paper.

◆ Wash and pick over the spinach and discard any tough stalks. Place on a clean tea towel, gather it up and shake it to dry.

◆ Roughly chop 140g/5oz of the salmon and cut the remainder into long strips and keep on one side.

◆ Put the chopped salmon, which must be very cold, and the eggs into a food processor or blender and reduce to a purée. With the machine running gradually add the spinach through the feed tube. (If you are using a blender you may have to stop it and add the spinach a few leaves at a time.) Keep the machine running until you have a thick purée then add, and just mix in, the chilled cream, nutmeg and seasonings. You will find that the spinach soaks up quite a lot of salt. Pour a third of the purée into the prepared tin, cover with half the strips of salmon, then layer with another third of purée, the remaining salmon strips and finally the last of the purée.

◆ Cover the terrine tightly with foil. Heat the oven to 160°C/325°F/gas 3. Put a deep baking tray into the oven with some small weights or a double layer of newspaper. This is to stop the base of the terrine cooking too fast. Put in the terrine and fill the tray to three-quarters with boiling water. Cook for an hour or until the terrine is set. Leave to cool.

TO FREEZE **Cover with foil or a double layer of cling film.**

TO DEFROST **Defrost overnight or for at least 15 hours in the fridge.**

TO MICROWAVE **Not suitable.**

TO FINISH **Turn the terrine out onto a dish and serve in slices with Tomato Vinaigrette or mayonnaise .**

❄ PROSCIUTTO AND PINENUT TARTLETS

The filling for these tartlets is a scrumptious mixture of goodies bound together with butter and breadcrumbs. I suggest making individual tartlets which look good and sophisticated as a first course. However you could also use a quiche tin to make one bigger tart which could be served as a light main course with a salad.

 You can easily tranform this into a vegetarian dish by leaving out the prosciutto and replacing it with a little more cheese, perhaps grated cheddar.

SERVES 6

FOR THE PASTRY

250g/9oz plain flour

1 teaspoon caster sugar

pinch salt

140g/5oz butter, cubed

1 egg yolk

cold water to mix

FOR THE FILLING

100g/3¹/₂oz white bread, hard crusts removed

2–3 cloves garlic

good bunch basil

50g/1³/₄oz parmesan, freshly grated

85g/3oz butter, cubed

70g/2¹/₂oz pinenuts

100g/3¹/₂oz prosciutto, chopped

Make the pastry by hand, or follow this method using a food processor.

◆ Put the flour, sugar and salt into a food processor and process to mix and lighten them. Add the butter and process until you reach the breadcrumb stage. Add the egg yolk and a tablespoon of cold water and process again until the pastry turns into a ball then stop the machine immediately. You may have to stop and dribble on a little more water.

◆ Take the pastry from the bowl and divide it into 6 even-sized pieces if making individual tartlets. Roll each piece into a ball, place them in a plastic bag and refrigerate for at least 30 minutes. Take the cold pastry from the fridge and to stop it cracking when rolled out, leave it on the side for 10-15 minutes.

◆ Roll each individual ball into a circle and line the tins, pushing the pastry well down the sides and then making a neat edge by rolling the pin over the top. Prick the bases with a fork then refrigerate.

◆ In a food processor or blender reduce the bread to crumbs then add the garlic and basil and process until they are also well chopped. Add the parmesan, the butter and some pepper and salt and process again until amalgamated. Finally add the pinenuts and chopped prosciutto and pulse the machine a few times to mix them in.

◆ Spoon the mixture into the pastry-lined tins and smooth evenly over the top.

▼ I give instructions for making the filling in a food processor or blender, but if you don't have one, grate the breadcrumbs and then, in a bowl, stir in the chopped ingredients one after another.

TO FREEZE **Place the tin or tins in a plastic bag or bags.**

TO DEFROST **I cook the tartlets from frozen but you could defrost them and then reduce the cooking time a little.**

TO MICROWAVE **Not suitable.**

TO COOK **Put an oven tray into the oven and heat it to 200°C/400°F/gas 6 then place the tart or tartlets on the hot tray and bake the tartlets for 20 minutes or a single tart for 25 minutes. Turn the oven down to 180°C/350°F/gas 4 and bake for a further 15–20 minutes or until the pastry is golden and the top bubbling and serve on a bed of green leaves.**

❄ CHICKEN LIVER TARTLETS

These chicken liver tartlets have a lovely crispy pastry and the filling is a light purée of chicken livers flavoured with sultanas and brandy. Tartlet tins come in various sizes; for a first course choose ones with a diameter of around 9-10cm/3½-4in but tins of 12cm/4½in diameter make tartlets big enough to serve with a salad for a light lunch. Conversely you could make smaller ones and either give everybody a couple or serve them alongside drinks. This recipe makes 6 large tartlets, 8 smaller ones and many more little ones.

SERVES 6–8

FOR THE PASTRY

250g/9oz plain flour

1 teaspoon caster sugar

pinch salt

140g/5oz butter, cubed

1 egg yolk

cold water to mix

FOR THE FILLING

2 tablespoons brandy

50g/1¾oz sultanas

250g/9oz chicken livers

50g/1¾oz butter

1 shallot, peeled and chopped

1 clove garlic, peeled and chopped

½ teaspoon fresh thyme

2 eggs

150ml/5fl oz double cream

Pour the brandy over the sultanas and leave to soak, preferably for 1-2 hours.

◆ Follow the instructions for Prosciutto and Pinenut Tartlets on page 38 to make the pastry and use it to line 6-8 tins. Refrigerate for 20 minutes or so.

◆ Put a baking sheet in the oven and preheat to 190°C/375°F/gas 5. Line each pastry-lined tartlet tin with a piece of crumpled foil, put them onto the hot sheet and cook for 10-12 minutes. Lower the temperature to 180°C/350°F/gas 4, remove the foil and bake them for a few minutes until golden in colour.

◆ To make the filling, pick over the chicken livers, remove any discoloured pieces and bits of membrane and then cut each liver into 3-4 pieces. Melt the butter in a frying pan and cook the shallot and garlic until soft then stir in the chicken livers and thyme and cook for a few minutes - the livers should be sealed on the outside but still slightly pink in the centre. Tip them into a food processor or blender and reduce to a purée. Break in the eggs and turn on the machine to mix them in. Pass the mixture through a sieve, squashing hard with a wooden spoon to push through as much as possible.

◆ Stir in the cream, the soaked sultanas and any remaining brandy and season well. Spoon the mixture into the pastry cases.

TO FREEZE **Cover each one with a piece of foil and when frozen pack the tartlets carefully into a plastic bag.**

TO DEFROST **Leave on the side for 3–4 hours or overnight in the fridge.**

TO MICROWAVE **Not suitable.**

TO REHEAT **Put into a preheated oven, 160°C/325°F/gas 3, for 20–25 minutes.**

TO SERVE **Serve warm, either alone or on a bed of mixed salad leaves.**

❄ PHEASANT AND GINGER TERRINE

This is one of the easiest and simplest terrines to which I have added ginger for extra interest and a good bite. The only fiddly part is taking the pheasant meat from the carcass - make sure your knife has a long sharp point. If pushed for time, you could of course ask your butcher to do it for you.

To allow the flavours to develop all terrines are best kept for a few hours before cooking. If you are using a fresh pheasant I would recommend freezing the terrine uncooked. It can then be slowly defrosted before cooking when it can be kept in the fridge for 4-5 days before being eaten. Once cut, it should be eaten within a couple of days.

If the pheasant or pork has previously been frozen it must be cooked before being frozen again. It will keep for up to a month in the freezer but to retain the texture and stop it becoming wet, defrost it very slowly in the fridge.

SERVES 6–8

1 pheasant, preferably fresh

3–4 juniper berries, lightly crushed

1 clove garlic, peeled and quartered

3 tablespoons green ginger wine

200g/7oz fresh fatty streaky pork

50g/1³/₄oz pistachio nuts

2 knobs stem ginger, peeled and diced

8–12 thin rashers streaky bacon

Strip the meat from the pheasant carcass, cutting out and discarding all the sinews. Cut the breasts into neat strips and reserve the rest of the meat.

◆ Put the juniper berries and garlic in a shallow dish with the ginger wine. Turn the strips of breast in the wine then cover with cling film and leave to marinate for at least 4 hours and preferably overnight.

◆ Drain and reserve the marinade, but discard the garlic and juniper berries. Roughly chop the streaky pork and reduce to a paste in a food processor or blender. Remove to a plate then put the reserved pheasant meat and up to half of the marinated breast strips into the food processor and chop them. Return the pork to the machine, add the reserved marinade and sprinkle on some salt and a good grinding of pepper then pulse the machine a few times to mix everything together. Heat a small frying pan and fry a teaspoon of the mixture. Taste and, if necessary add more salt and pepper to the main mixture then transfer it to a bowl and stir in the pistachio nuts and the diced ginger.

◆ Line a terrine (or a soufflé dish) with the streaky bacon, leaving the ends to drape over the sides. It should be very thin; you may need to stretch it out on a chopping board with the back of a knife. Spoon about half the pork mixture into the terrine then lay the strips of breast over it. Cover with the remaining pork mixture then pull the bacon ends over the top. The terrine should be covered with bacon; you may need another rasher.

TO FREEZE **If using fresh pheasant and pork, freeze immediately covered with a sheet of foil. With frozen pheasant, you must cook the terrine first following the instructions below and freeze when cold.**

TO DEFROST **The terrine, cooked or not, should be defrosted very slowly in the fridge. It will take at least 24 hours.**

TO MICROWAVE **Not suitable.**

TO COOK **Heat the oven to 160°C/325°F/ gas 3 and boil a kettle of water. Lay two or three sheets of folded newspaper in the centre of a deep roasting pan and pour in the boiling water then place the terrine, fresh or defrosted, on the newspaper which will prevent the bottom cooking too quickly. The water should come at least halfway up the sides of the terrine. Bake for 1³/₄–2 hours then leave it to cool in the oven for around 20 minutes. Refrigerate when cold.**

TO SERVE **Accompany it with hot toast, unsalted butter and some gherkins or crunchy radishes on the side.**

❄ OYSTERS

One of my recent discoveries is that fresh oysters can be frozen. This is buying ahead rather than cooking ahead but I think it qualifies for this book as so many people regard oysters as a real treat, and also if you buy them in quantity the price becomes more reasonable.

SERVES 6–8

72 oysters

TO FINISH
wedges of lemon
sprinkling cayenne

There is nothing to do in advance but consult with your guests to make sure that everybody is happy to eat oysters. If they are they will feel truly spoiled. Although the quantity of oysters may seem a lot, I rarely find any are left over.

TO FREEZE **Freeze the fresh oysters in double plastic bags the moment you get them home.**

TO DEFROST **Place them in a dish or on a tray, flat side up, and defrost in the fridge for 7–8 hours. You want them to be wholly defrosted but don't keep them for too long before eating.**

TO MICROWAVE **Not suitable.**

TO FINISH **Use an oyster knife or sturdy kitchen knife to open the shells. This should not be too much of a struggle as freezing will have relaxed the clamping muscle. Hold them concave side down to preserve the juices and make sure that you cut the oysters free from the shells. Eat them *au nature*, or with wedges of lemon or a light sprinkling of cayenne, accompanied with brown bread and butter.**

fish

Over the past few years fish has come into its own as people have realised that not only is it one of the healthiest foods available but it is also one that titillates the tastebuds in the most subtle of ways. The recipes included here for fish pies and fish in sauces can all be made with either fresh or frozen fish and all of them make very good, satisfying main courses. For the other recipes I have chosen the quick option of using fresh fish, placed with vegetables and a sauce or a marinade into a freezer- and ovenproof serving dish which is then covered and frozen. Slow defrosting in the fridge allows the sauce or marinade ingredients to fuse together and then all that needs to be done is to put the dish into a pre-heated oven and bake it for around half an hour or until the fish is just cooked. It is difficult to tell from the taste that the fish and sauce have spent a week or two in the freezer and nothing could be simpler for the host or hostess.

❄ SEAFOOD-FILLED GOUGERE

A gougère is a ring of choux pastry with a savoury filling which makes a very good freezer dish. The pastry is piped or spooned round the edge of a shallow freezer- and ovenproof dish, the filling spooned into the centre and the dish immediately frozen. I have tried both defrosting the gougère before cooking it and cooking it from frozen, and the pastry is lighter and rises better when it is taken from the freezer and put straight into a hot oven.

The filling I give is definitely a party one with the sweet flavour of the scallops combining well with the Mediterranean-type fish.

SERVES 4 AS A MAIN COURSE, 6 AS A STARTER

FOR THE FILLING
85g/3oz squid
85g/3oz calamari
150ml/5fl oz dry white wine
175g/6oz scallops
85g/3oz prawns, peeled
25g/1oz butter
25g/1oz flour
2 teaspoons brandy
4 tablespoons double cream

FOR THE CHOUX PASTRY
115g/4oz flour
1/2 teaspoon salt
200ml/7fl oz water
75g/2³/₄oz butter
3 eggs
bunch chives, snipped
50g/1³/₄oz gruyère, grated

Slice the squid into rounds and cut the calamari rings in half. Put them both into a pan with the wine, 400ml/14fl oz of water and a little salt, bring to the boil and simmer gently for 25-30 minutes or until the seafood is tender. Slice the scallops, putting the corals on one side and add them with the prawns and cook for a further 2 minutes. Remove from the heat, stir in the scallop corals then drain off and reserve the liquid.

◆ Melt the butter, stir in the flour then add the cooking liquid and the brandy and bring to the boil. Cook for 5 minutes then stir in the cream and season to taste. Take from the heat and add the seafood. Leave, stirring occasionally, until cool.

◆ Next, make the pastry. Sift the flour and salt together onto a piece of paper. Put the water and butter into a pan and heat slowly until the butter has melted then turn up the heat and bring the mixture quickly to the boil. Remove the pan from the heat and immediately, using the paper as a funnel, tip in all the flour. Beat with a wooden spoon to amalgamate the mixture then return the pan to the heat and beat the dough for 1/2 minute or so until it has dried a little and started to form a crust on the bottom of the pan. Take the pan from the heat and leave until tepid.

◆ Turn the dough into a food processor (easiest), or into a bowl and use an electric whisk. Whisk the eggs lightly together and with the machine running add them slowly through the feed tube. You may not need to use all the egg but you need to finish with a smooth shiny dough that falls from a spoon with a good plop when lightly shaken. When you have reached the right consistency add the snipped chives, cheese and seasoning.

◆ Butter a good-sized shallow freezer- and ovenproof dish well and use a wet spoon or a piping bag to put mounds of the pastry all round the edge. Spoon the seafood and sauce into the centre.

TO FREEZE **Cover with foil or a double layer of cling film.**
TO DEFROST **Cook the gougère from frozen.**
TO MICROWAVE **Not suitable.**
TO COOK **Preheat the oven to 220°C/425°F/gas 7 and bake the gougère for 35–40 minutes or until the pastry has puffed up and is golden brown.**

❄ SMOKED HADDOCK PIE

This pie is more for family, or close friends and a kitchen supper than to be shown off in the dining room, but it's a good one with smoked haddock and prawns and, breaking all the rules, hard-boiled eggs. I was agreeably surprised that the eggs withstood the freezing but I would add that they must be well chopped and well covered with the sauce and that the pie should probably not be frozen for more than a week or two.

The addition of cream for the sauce is optional, but if this is for friends or a party, add it. The amount makes little difference to the fat content of the pie and quite a lot to the taste.

SERVES 6

450g/1lb smoked haddock

1 onion

4 sticks celery, preferably inside ones

700ml/1¼ pints milk

50g/1³⁄₄oz butter

50g/1³⁄₄oz flour

4 tablespoons cream (optional)

50g/1³⁄₄oz cheddar, grated

large bunch parsley, chopped

4 hard-boiled eggs, finely chopped

175g/6oz peeled prawns

FOR THE TOPPING

500g/1lb 2oz potatoes

1 egg yolk

2 tablespoons milk

50g/1³⁄₄oz butter

2 tablespoons cream (optional)

25g/1oz cheddar, grated

Put the haddock into a large saucepan with the peeled and quartered onion and 1 stick of celery. Cover with the milk and bring slowly to the boil. Simmer for 2 minutes then remove the pan from the heat and leave to cool a little before flaking the fish. Strain and reserve the milk. (You could, if you prefer, cook the fish in the microwave.)

◆ Chop the remaining sticks of celery, put them into a pan of salted boiling water and cook until tender. Drain and reserve.

◆ In a large pan melt the butter, stir in the flour and cook for 1-2 minutes before pouring in the reserved milk. Stirring, bring the sauce to the boil and let it simmer and cook for 2-3 minutes then take the pan from the heat and add the cream, the cheese and the chopped parsley and season, remembering that the fish may be rather salty. Finally, add the fish together with the celery, the chopped hard-boiled eggs and the prawns and gently stir them all in.

◆ Turn the fish mixture into a large pie or serving dish and leave until cold.

◆ While the pie is cooling cook the potatoes and mash them until smooth. Whisk the egg yolk into the milk and lightly beat them in together with the butter and cream, if using. Add the cheese and season to taste. Spread the potato evenly over the pie and score it with the tines of a fork.

TO FREEZE **Cover with foil or a double layer of cling film.**

TO DEFROST **Leave on the side for 8–10 hours or in the fridge for up to 24 hours.**

TO MICROWAVE **Not suitable.**

TO REHEAT **Heat in the oven set to 190°C/375°F/gas 5 for 40 minutes or until the top is brown and bubbling.**

❄ MEEN MOLEE (FISH IN A COCONUT AND CHILLI SAUCE)

Meen Molee – meen is a Tamil word for fish – is a favourite dish of southern India and especially Cochin in Kerala where Tamil is spoken. The dish dates from the Raj and was later taken up by the British in India. It became a great favourite but the memsahibs gradually dispensed with most or all of of the chilli, and the dish became rather insipid. This recipe retains some of the original bite but is nothing like as hot as the dish you would be served in Kerala; however you can always add extra chillies.

You can perfectly well drink a rustic wine with this dish, but if you add further chillies you might prefer a glass of lager.

SERVES 6

1kg/2lb 4oz fresh monkfish tails (boned and skinned to weigh 650–700g/1lb 7oz–1lb 9oz)

1 teaspoon turmeric

juice $^1/_2$ lime

3 green chillies

3 medium onions

7cm/2$^3/_4$in piece ginger

4 cloves garlic

3 tomatoes, peeled

3 tablespoons sunflower oil

4 cardamom pods

5 peppercorns

140g/5oz creamed coconut

Cut the fish into good-sized chunks. In a flat dish combine $^1/_2$ teaspoon turmeric with 1 teaspoon salt and the lime juice. Add the fish, turn it in the mixture then leave to marinate for $^1/_2$ hour.

◆ Carefully (I wear rubber gloves) top, tail, deseed and roughly chop the chillies. Peel and roughly chop 1 onion and half the ginger. Peel the garlic cloves and remove any centre shoots. Put all these into a blender or food processor, add 1 tablespoon of water, reduce to a paste then keep until needed.

◆ Peel and finely slice the remaining onions and keep on one side. Deseed and chop the peeled tomatoes and peel and finely slice the rest of the ginger and keep separately on one side.

◆ With a slotted spoon remove the fish to a plate lined with a double layer of kitchen paper and pat with more paper to remove all moisture. In a wok or wide pan heat 1 tablespoon of oil then throw in the fish and toss it for around 30 seconds just to seal it. Remove from the pan and keep on one side.

◆ Wipe the pan clean, return it to the hob, add the remaining oil then gently cook the sliced onions until softened. Add the tomatoes, sliced ginger, cardamoms and peppercorns and cook, stirring, for 1-2 minutes before adding the chilli and onion paste. Cook for a further 2 minutes then add 60g/2$^1/_4$oz of the creamed coconut, well chopped or crumbled, the remaining turmeric, a sprinkling of salt and 200ml/7fl oz water. Still stirring, cook until the coconut has melted and the sauce is bubbling. Take from the heat and leave until cold.

◆ Dissolve the remaining creamed coconut in 100ml/3$^1/_2$fl oz hot water, add to the cooled sauce, then gently stir in the reserved fish.

TO FREEZE Turn into a freezer- and oven-proof dish and cover or into a rigid freezer container.

TO DEFROST Leave on the side for at least 7 hours or in the fridge for 18 hours.

TO MICROWAVE Cover with cling film and follow your microwave instructions for defrosting and cooking.

TO COOK Cover the dish with foil and put it in the oven heated to 180°C/350°F/gas 4 for 35–40 minutes or until the sauce starts to bubble and the fish is just cooked. Taste the sauce and, if necessary, add more salt.

TO SERVE Serve with plain boiled or steamed basmati rice and, if liked, some crispy poppadums or naan bread.

❄ EXTRA-SPECIAL FISH PIE

This fish pie is stuffed with goodies and makes a very useful one-dish main course, needing only a crunchy green salad on the side. Salmon and prawns with mushrooms are the main ingredients but the sauce, with herbs, wine and a few spoonfuls of mayonnaise, is really something special.

SERVES 6

200ml/7fl oz milk

few parsley stalks, bay leaf, sage leaf and 4 peppercorns

500g/1lb 2oz salmon fillet

65g/2^1/$_2$oz butter

2 spring onions, chopped

40g/1^1/$_2$oz flour

150ml/5fl oz dry white wine

few sprigs tarragon, chopped

1 tablespoon parsley, chopped

100g/3^1/$_2$oz mayonnaise

100g/3^1/$_2$oz mushrooms

150g/5^1/$_2$oz prawns, defrosted, if frozen

FOR THE TOPPING

750g/1lb 10oz potatoes

1 egg yolk

3 tablespoons milk

3 tablespoons cream

75g/2^3/$_2$oz butter

Pour the milk into a pan and add the parsley stalks, the bay leaf, sage leaf and peppercorns. Bring the milk just to boiling point then remove the pan from the heat and leave the milk and herbs to infuse for 30 minutes or so.

◆ Smear the salmon with 25g/1oz butter and cook it either in the microwave according to your model's instructions or in a foil packet in the oven for 20 minutes at 180°C/350°F/gas 4. Leave to cool, reserve any juices, then remove the skin, debone and flake the fish.

◆ In a large pan melt the remaining butter, stir in the spring onions and cook them for 2-3 minutes. Stir in the flour and cook for a further minute before stirring in the wine then the strained milk and juices from the salmon. Continue to stir, bring it to the boil and gently simmer for 3-4 minutes. Take the pan from the heat and leave to cool slightly before stirring in the tarragon and the parsley and the mayonnaise. Season to taste. Destalk the mushrooms, cut them into thin slices and add them, the salmon and prawns to the sauce.

◆ Turn the fish mixture into a large pie dish or similar and leave until cold.

◆ While the pie is cooling cook the potatoes and mash them until smooth. Whisk the egg yolk into the milk and cream, and beat them into the potatoes with the butter. Spread the potato onto the pie and score the top with the tines of a fork.

TO FREEZE **Cover with foil or a double layer of cling film.**

TO DEFROST **Leave in the refrigerator overnight or preferably for 24 hours.**

TO MICROWAVE **Not suitable.**

TO REHEAT **Heat in a moderate oven, 180°C/350°F/gas 4, for 45 minutes then raise the heat and cook for a few minutes until the top is golden brown.**

TO SERVE **Serve with crisp green leaves.**

BAKED COD WITH LENTILS AND LEEKS

Lentils marry remarkably well with a solid white fish and for this recipe I have used cod but you could perfectly well replace it with haddock. This is an adaptation for the freezer of a recipe that appears in *The French Recipe Book* by Carole Clements and Elizabeth Wolf-Cohen.

SERVES 6

250g/9oz Puy lentils

clove garlic, peeled and crushed

2.5cm/1in piece ginger, peeled and finely chopped

1 teaspoon sugar

1 tablespoon wine vinegar

10 tablespoons olive oil

zest 1 orange

1 teaspoon ground cumin

450g/1lb leeks

6 fresh cod steaks or 800–900g/1lb 12oz–2lb skinless cod fillet

Wash the lentils and put them into a pan with the garlic, ginger, sugar and vinegar and add enough water to cover by 5cm/2in. Bring to the boil then cover the pan and leave it to simmer for 25-35 minutes or until the lentils are tender but not mushy. While they cook, stir them a few times and, if necessary, add a little more water. Drain the lentils and stir in 6 tablespoons of olive oil, the orange zest, the ground cumin and season. Keep on one side.

◆ Split the leeks almost down to the base, wash them well then slice. Put the remaining oil into a pan, add the leeks and a small amount of water. Bring to simmering point and cook gently, adding more water if necessary, until the leeks are tender and the liquid has evaporated. Season to taste.

TO FREEZE **Spoon the lentils into a shallow freezer- and ovenproof dish and allow to cool. Top with the pieces of fish and cover with the cooled leeks. Cover the dish with foil or a double layer of cling film.**

TO DEFROST **Leave in the fridge for up to 24 hours.**

TO MICROWAVE **Follow your microwave instructions for defrosting and cooking.**

TO COOK **Bake the covered dish for 30 minutes at 190°C/375°F/gas 5 or until everything is hot and the fish is cooked.**

❄ FISH CAKES

Fish cakes are not considered dinner party fare but properly made ones, presented well, are still very popular. These are made half and half with smoked and fresh cod which, with lots of parsley and chives, make as good a fish cake as any. They freeze beautifully and you need only defrost the number you think you need - but remember they are very moreish!

MAKES 10–12 FISH CAKES

450g/1lb floury potatoes

225g/8oz fresh cod fillet

milk to cook the fish

225g/8oz smoked cod

25g/1oz butter

2 tablespoons parsley, finely chopped

2 tablespoons chives, snipped

3 tablespoons flour

2 eggs, beaten

about 115g/4oz breadcrumbs

Peel the potatoes and boil in a pan of salted water. While they cook, put the fresh cod into a sauté pan, cover with milk and bring to the boil. Simmer for 1 minute, then use a slotted spoon to remove the fish. Put the smoked cod into the milk, bring back to simmering point and cook for 2-3 minutes, until just cooked, before taking it from the heat. Flake both pieces of fish, removing any skin or bones.

◆ When the potatoes are soft, drain and mash them until very smooth, adding the butter and herbs. Finally, fold the flaked fish into the potato mixture and season well.

◆ To make the fish cakes you will need three small bowls, one filled with flour, the second with the beaten eggs and the third with the breadcrumbs.

◆ Flour your hands and take some of the mixture and shape it into an individual cake. Dip it into the flour, then the egg and finally into the breadcrumbs. Repeat until you have used up all the mixture.

TO FREEZE **Place the fish cakes on a tray and freeze. When they are frozen remove them to a bag for storage.**

TO DEFROST **Defrost for 2–3 hours in the fridge or cook from frozen.**

TO MICROWAVE **Not suitable.**

TO COOK **Heat a little oil and a knob of butter in a frying pan and fry the fish cakes, turning once or twice, until they are hot and golden brown. Drain well on kitchen paper.**

FISH CAKES WITH BRAISED CHICORY (PAGE 128)

❄ COD WITH TOMATO, OLIVE AND CAPER SAUCE AND HOT GARLIC OIL

The humble cod has recently been rediscovered and can now be found on the menus of the very best restaurants. For this dish the raw cod is covered with a tasty Mediterranean sauce and immediately frozen. While defrosting the flavours seem to seep into the fish, which is then baked, taken from the oven and, just before eating, drizzled with hot and garlicky olive oil. Simple and good, but do use fresh and not frozen fish.

SERVES 6

6 medium tomatoes, peeled

4 tablespoons olive oil

½ Spanish onion, peeled and finely chopped

3 pieces sun-dried tomatoes, chopped

200g/7oz can green olives stuffed with anchovies, drained

2 tablespoons capers, rinsed

small bunch flat-leaf parsley, roughly chopped

6 fresh cod steaks or 800–900g/1lb 12oz–2lb skinless cod fillet

TO FINISH

2 cloves garlic, peeled and crushed

2 tablespoons olive oil

Quarter each tomato, deseed and cut each quarter into 3-4 pieces. Heat 2 tablespoons of the olive oil and gently sauté the onion until very soft.

◆ Add the tomatoes, sun-dried tomatoes, olives, capers, and parsley. Cook everything for just 1 minute then cool.

◆ Put the cod steaks into a shallow freezer- and ovenproof dish and pour over the cooled sauce.

TO FREEZE **Cover tightly with foil or a double layer of cling film.**

TO DEFROST **Leave on the side for 5–6 hours or overnight in the fridge.**

TO MICROWAVE **Follow your microwave instructions for defrosting and cooking then finish as below.**

TO COOK **Put in the oven at 180°C/350°F/ gas 4 for 25–30 minutes or until the fish is just cooked.**

TO FINISH **Just before serving put the garlic cloves and olive oil in a saucepan and heat. Keep the heat low: do not let the garlic brown. Strain the hot olive oil over the fish and serve at once.**

❄ FISH FLORENTINE

A well-known dish that freezes beautifully. Eat it for a main course with some new potatoes on the side, or, served in smaller quantities, for a first course. It is quite rich and does taste much nicer when made with the cream and egg yolk, but you could leave them out. As the fish is not cooked before freezing make sure that you use fresh fish.

SERVES 6

750g/1lb 10oz fresh spinach

50g/1³/₄oz butter plus extra for greasing

75ml/2¹/₂fl oz double cream plus extra 3 tablespoons

scraping nutmeg

1kg/2lb 4oz fresh sole, lemon sole or plaice fillets, skinned

25g/1oz flour

350ml/12fl oz milk

20g/³/₄oz parmesan, grated

20g/³/₄oz gruyère, grated

1 egg yolk

Wash the spinach well, discarding any tough stalks, then put into a large pan and place over a medium heat. Cook, turning the leaves from time to time, until they are melted. When the spinach is cooked drain in a colander and leave to cool. Use your hands to squeeze out the water then put the spinach in a food processor together with half the butter and the 3 tablespoons of cream. Reduce to a purée and season to taste with salt, pepper and a scraping of nutmeg.

◆ Grease a gratin dish well and spread the purée over the bottom. Arrange the fish fillets over the top; depending on the size of the dish, you may have to put them in two layers.

◆ To make the sauce melt the remaining butter in a pan, stir in the flour and cook briefly before adding the milk. Bring to the boil and whisk until you have a smooth sauce. Cook for 2-3 minutes then take from the heat and stir in the cream, the cheeses and finally the egg yolk. Season with salt, pepper and a little nutmeg. Pour the sauce over the fish fillets, making sure that the whole dish is covered.

TO FREEZE **Cover with foil.**

TO DEFROST **Leave in the fridge for at least 8–10 hours.**

TO MICROWAVE **Follow your microwave instructions for defrosting and cooking, remembering that the fish has to be cooked, not simply reheated.**

TO COOK **Put the foil-covered dish in the oven at 180°C/350°F/gas 4 for 30–35 minutes. Brown the top by removing the foil for the last 20 minutes. This dish can also be cooked from frozen or partially defrosted in a low oven, 160°C/325°F/gas 3. It will take considerably longer; the exact time depending on how frozen it is. Check that the fish is fully cooked before serving.**

TO SERVE **Delicious with boiled and seasoned new potatoes.**

❄ SEA BREAM WITH FENNEL AND ORANGE STUFFING

There is something dramatic and satisfactory about serving a whole fish, but for 6 people you would need a big one, of a size that is difficult to obtain, so I am inclined to produce this as a special dish when there are just 4 of us. You could, of course, double it up for 8.

I will use sea bass as often as sea bream and people will tell you that it is a great pity to freeze such good fish and, yes, you could always make and freeze the fennel accompaniment, and after defrosting spread it round a fresh fish. However, provided everything is wrapped carefully in a double layer of foil, frozen very quickly and kept for no more than 2 weeks, I find that there is no deterioration in the result and this recipe is totally trouble-free when it comes to defrosting and cooking the fish.

The addition of a spoonful of Pernod is good but it will accentuate the anise flavour and you may prefer to leave it out.

SERVES 4

1 fresh sea bream or sea bass of around 1.6kg/3lb 8oz

3 tablespoons olive oil

2 large fennel bulbs, trimmed and thinly sliced

2 shallots, peeled and sliced

1–2 cloves garlic, peeled and finely chopped

150ml/5fl oz dry white wine

zest ¹/₂ orange and juice 1 orange

zest and juice ¹/₂ lemon

3 star anise

1 tablespoon Pernod (optional)

Get your fishmonger to cut the fins from the fish, descale and gut it.
◆ Pour the olive oil into a sauté pan and add all the other ingredients except for the fish and the Pernod. Bring to the boil, cover and simmer gently for 15 minutes or until the fennel is soft and much of the liquid has evaporated. Season to taste and stir in the Pernod. Leave to cool.
◆ Stuff the fish with some of the fennel mixture. Lay out, one on top of the other, two large sheets of foil, brush the top one with oil and spoon half the remaining fennel mixture onto it. Lay the fish on the top and spread the remaining fennel mixture over it. Turn in the ends of the top sheet of foil, then bring up the sides and seal them. Repeat with the second sheet.

TO FREEZE **Put the prepared parcel into the freezer.**

TO DEFROST **Leave in the fridge for up to 24 hours.**

TO MICROWAVE **Not suitable.**

TO COOK **Put the defrosted parcel into a heated oven at 180°C/350°F/gas 4 for 45 minutes or until the fish is just cooked.**

TO FINISH **Open the parcel and carefully lift the fish onto a large platter. Skin if you wish. Spoon the fennel and juices round it, discarding the star anise.**

TO SERVE **I like to serve the fish with new potatoes followed by a large green salad.**

❄ SALMON WITH SALSA VERDE

The remaining recipes in this section are very easy ones in which the salmon fillets or steaks are frozen along with a piquant sauce which is also used as a marinade. They are also trouble-free, as there is no last-minute attention - once the dish is defrosted all it needs is baking in the oven. I give recipes for three different sauces, all of them good and all suitable for this treatment. For a large party it would be fun to use both the red salsa (Salsa Rossa on page 57) and this green salsa and arrange the salmon steaks in alternating colours on the serving dish (see photograph on page 2).

Salsa verde, the best known of the Italian salsas, is a fresh herb and olive oil sauce which in Italy would always be made with whatever was available in the garden then sharpened up, or not, depending on the food it was to accompany. Strong flavours complement rather than overpower salmon so this recipe for salsa verde has the addition of anchovy fillets, vinegar and capers, but if you like something milder reduce the amounts I suggest. Flat-leaf parsley is essential but you could replace the rocket with either dill or tarragon. Salsa is easiest made in a food processor but otherwise chop the herbs and garlic and then mix everything together.

SERVES 6

1 clove garlic

good bunch of flat-leaf parsley

4–5 leaves rocket

about 20g/³/₄oz ciabatta or similar bread, sliced

4 anchovy fillets, rinsed

1 tablespoon red wine vinegar

6 tablespoons olive oil

1 tablespoon capers, rinsed

6 fresh salmon steaks or pieces of fillet, skinned

Chop the garlic clove in the food processor then add the herbs and the bread and reduce to a purée. Roughly chop the anchovy fillets and add together with the vinegar and olive oil and process until everything has amalgamated. Season with pepper and, if necessary, salt, add the capers and turn the machine on again very briefly to mix everything together.

◆ Smear some of the salsa over the bottom of a freezer- and ovenproof dish large enough to take the salmon in a single layer. Put the salmon in the dish and spoon over the rest of the salsa.

TO FREEZE **Cover with foil or a double layer of cling film.**

TO DEFROST **Leave for 5–6 hours on the side or for 15 hours in the fridge.**

TO MICROWAVE **Defrost and cook the salmon in your microwave following the instructions for your oven.**

TO COOK **Heat the oven to 180°C/ 350°F/gas 4. Keep the dish covered with foil and bake the defrosted salmon for 25–30 minutes or until just cooked.**

SALMON WITH SALSA ROSSA

This version of salsa combines the sweetness of red pepper with the tang of tomato and everything is pepped up with chilli and garlic. (See photograph on page 2).

SERVES 6

2 red peppers, quartered, deseeded and cored

½ small red chilli, or less depending on heat

1 shallot

1 clove garlic

3 tablespoons olive oil

400g/14oz can peeled whole or chopped plum tomatoes

6 fresh salmon steaks or pieces of fillet, skinned

Put the pepper quarters, skin side up, on a sheet of foil under a hot grill. Grill until the skin is blackened and charred. Put the hot peppers into a plastic bag, seal the end and leave to steam for around 20 minutes, then remove the peppers from the bag, peel off the skins and cut the flesh into short strips.

◆ Halve the chilli, remove the seeds and roughly chop it. Peel and chop the shallot and the garlic clove. Heat the oil and over a low flame sauté the chilli, shallot and garlic until soft. Add the peppers and tomatoes and simmer very gently for ½ hour to allow the flavours to amalgamate. Pour the cooked sauce into a food processor and reduce to a purée and season to taste. If the salsa seems to be too thick, stir in another 1-2 tablespoons of olive oil.

◆ Smear some of the salsa over the bottom of a freezer- and ovenproof dish, large enough to take the salmon in a single layer. Put the salmon in the dish and spoon over the rest of the salsa.

TO FREEZE, TO DEFROST, TO MICROWAVE AND TO COOK **Follow the instructions for Salmon with Salsa Verde (opposite).**

SALMON WITH CHERMOULA

SERVES 6

bunch coriander, chopped

6 tablespoons olive oil

2 cloves garlic, peeled and finely chopped

1 teaspoon ground cumin

1 teaspoon paprika

½ teaspoon ground coriander

1cm/½in root ginger, peeled and finely chopped

pinch cayenne

zest and juice 1 lime

6 fresh salmon steaks or pieces of fillet, skinned

Mix together all the ingredients apart from the salmon, and season to taste.

◆ Smear some of the chermoula over the bottom of a freezer- and ovenproof dish large enough to take the salmon in a single layer. Put the salmon in the dish and spoon over the rest of the chermoula.

TO FREEZE, TO DEFROST, TO MICROWAVE AND TO COOK **Follow the instructions for Salmon with Salsa Verde (opposite).**

❄ STUFFED PAUPIETTES OF SOLE IN A PRAWN SAUCE

For something special use fillets of sole but large fillets of lemon sole or plaice are a good substitute. The amounts I give are enough for the stuffing and sauce for a main course when you will need to use 2 fillets per person. However this dish is also good served as a first course – allow, say, 1 fillet per person and reduce the amounts for the sauce and stuffing. The fish need to be skinned and filleted but that is a job for your friendly fishmonger.

SERVES 6

60g/2$^{1}/_{4}$oz butter

1 shallot, peeled and finely chopped

200g/7oz prawns or shrimps, peeled

1 tablespoon parsley, chopped

75g/2$^{3}/_{4}$oz fresh breadcrumbs, moistened in a little milk

12 fresh fillets of sole, lemon sole or plaice, skinned

50g/1$^{3}/_{4}$oz flour

500ml/18fl oz milk

1 egg yolk

200ml/7fl oz double cream

Melt a knob of the butter and gently sauté the shallot until it is soft. Very roughly chop 75g/2$^{3}/_{4}$oz of the prawns. Mix the shallot, prawns and parsley into the breadcrumbs and season to taste. Put a spoonful onto each fish fillet and roll up. Lay the stuffed fillets in a well-greased freezer- and ovenproof gratin dish.

◆ Melt the remaining butter, stir in the flour and then slowly add the milk. Keep stirring until you have a smooth sauce then take it from the heat and leave it to cool a little. Whisk the egg yolk and cream together and stir into the sauce. Season to taste then add the remaining prawns. Cool then pour the sauce over the fish.

TO FREEZE **Cover with foil or a double layer of cling film.**

TO DEFROST **Leave in the fridge for 18–24 hours.**

TO MICROWAVE **Follow your microwave instructions for defrosting and cooking.**

TO COOK **Bake the foil-covered dish in the oven at 180°C/350°F/gas 4 for 25–30 minutes or until the fish is just cooked.**

poultry & game

In this chapter I give recipes using several different types of poultry and game but chicken predominates since there are so many interesting ways to cook it. I feel strongly about battery-raised chickens which have no quality of life and no flavour so would encourage you to use free-range birds. In several of the recipes I have only lightly cooked the poultry joints before freezing. This is a method that works well and saves you from serving up an overcooked and quite possibly tasteless bird. However, this method should only be used for fresh, not frozen and defrosted joints. If you are going to use meat that has already been frozen you must then cook it very thoroughly before freezing. Remember that salmonella is found in poultry joints, so you must make absolutely sure in these recipes that the entire casserole, the poultry and the sauce, are completely defrosted before you reheat it. I often give instructions for reheating the dishes at a low temperature for quite a long time which leads to a more succulent and tender bird than one given a quick blast in a hot oven.

❄ SAUTE OF CHICKEN WITH RED WINE VINEGAR, TOMATO AND GARLIC

In the Middle Ages, before lemons were available, the French discovered that using vinegar gave many dishes a certain acidity and a nice sharpness. This recipe doesn't have its origins quite so far back as it also uses tomatoes, which were introduced at a later date. However, it is a good dish that has stood the test of time and often features, in one form or another, in recipe books. I like this simple version: the vinegar, cooked and reduced, is not at all overpowering and the tomatoes and well-cooked garlic give the sauce a nice sweetness. Use the best quality red wine vinegar you can find.

SERVES 6

8–10 plump cloves garlic, peeled and halved

1.8–2kg/4–4 ¹⁄₂lb fresh free-range chicken, jointed into 6 pieces, or 6 fresh free-range chicken joints

75g/2³⁄₄oz butter

300ml/¹⁄₂ pint red wine vinegar

700g/1lb 9oz ripe tomatoes, skinned, deseeded and chopped

400g/14oz can chopped tomatoes

300ml/10fl oz chicken stock

TO FINISH
handful parsley, chopped

Remove any centre shoots from the garlic.

◆ Dry the chicken joints with kitchen paper and season them lightly.

◆ In a large lidded sauté pan heat the butter until it foams. Add the chicken pieces and fry, turning them occasionally until well browned. Turn them skin side up and add the garlic. Cover the pan, reduce the heat and leave to cook for 5 minutes. Then use the lid to hold back the chicken and garlic and drain off the fat.

◆ Return the pan to the heat, pour in the vinegar and simmer uncovered, turning the chicken once or twice, until the liquid has reduced to 2-3 tablespoons. Add the tomatoes, cover the pan and simmer gently for 10 minutes. Remove the chicken, add the stock, season lightly and simmer for a further 5 minutes or until the sauce has thickened. Remove and reserve the garlic with the chicken then sieve the sauce, pressing hard to extract all the juice from the tomatoes. Leave until cold.

TO FREEZE **Put everything into a freezer- and ovenproof casserole or pour the sauce into a rigid freezer container then add the garlic and the chicken.**

TO DEFROST **Leave on the side for 10–12 hours or for at least 18 hours in the fridge. Make sure that the chicken is completely defrosted.**

TO MICROWAVE **Follow your microwave instructions to defrost and reheat.**

TO REHEAT **Heat in the oven at 160°C/ 325°F/gas 3 for 50 minutes to 1 hour.**

TO FINISH **Sprinkle the parsley evenly over the top and when serving make sure that everybody gets some garlic.**

❄ SUPREMES OF CHICKEN IN WHITE WINE AND MUSHROOM SAUCE

Another very traditional French dish, this one is made of the breast or *suprêmes* of chicken and mushrooms in a velouté sauce. The sauce is not difficult to make but to achieve real depth and flavour you need to use really good strong home-made chicken stock.

I prefer to make this dish with boneless breasts of free-range chicken, which can be on the large side – if so, 4 chicken breasts may be enough for 6 people.

The amount of cream you use is up to you, but the sauce will taste rather thin if you leave it out altogether.

SERVES 6

4 –6 fresh free-range chicken breasts, skinned and boned

450ml/16fl oz home-made chicken stock

90g/3¼oz butter

250g/9oz mushrooms, peeled and sliced

juice ½ lemon

50g/1¾oz flour

150ml/5fl.oz dry white wine

30–75ml/1–2½fl.oz double cream

1 tablespoon parsley, chopped

Using a sharp knife cut each chicken breast, at an angle, into 3-4 medium slices.

◆ Pour the stock into a sauté pan, bring it up to simmering point, put in the chicken and poach for about 5 minutes or until just tender. Remove the chicken with a slotted spoon and pour the stock into a small bowl.

◆ Melt half the butter in a frying pan, add the mushrooms, squeeze in the lemon juice, cook and stir for 3-4 minutes or until the mushrooms are tender, then turn them onto a plate.

◆ Melt the remaining butter in the sauté pan, stir in the flour and cook 1-2 minutes or until the roux darkens in colour. Slowly, still stirring, pour in the reserved stock, then the wine. Bring to the boil and let it simmer for 4-5 minutes before adding the cream and seasoning to taste. Take the pan from the heat and stir in the chicken, mushrooms and parsley.

◆ Spoon everything into a shallow freezer- and ovenproof dish and leave until cold.

TO FREEZE **Cover with foil.**
TO DEFROST **Leave on the side for 6–7 hours or in the fridge for 15 hours.**
TO MICROWAVE **Follow your microwave instructions to defrost and reheat.**
TO REHEAT **Heat the oven to 160°C/325°F/gas 3 and cook the foil-covered dish for 50 minutes.**

❄ SUMMER CHICKEN PROVENCAL

A lovely Provençal dish, perfect for those long, hot, hazy days of summer. Use a selection of different coloured peppers, which not only add to the look but also bring a variety of tastes. If you can find one, a few strips of the 'hot' orange pepper would add bite; otherwise I like to stir in a few chilli flakes.

SERVES 6

4–5 peppers, red, yellow and orange, halved and deseeded

6 tablespoons olive oil

6 fresh free-range chicken breasts with the bone in

4 pieces sun-dried tomato, soaked in a little water

1 large Spanish onion, peeled and sliced thinly

12–16 black olives, stoned

1/2 teaspoon chilli flakes (optional)

TO COOK

2 cloves garlic

a little olive oil

Lay the peppers, skin side up, on a grill pan on a piece of foil. Grill until the skin is black and blistered, turning if necessary, then put them in a plastic bag and seal it. Leave until the peppers are cool then remove the skin and cut the flesh into strips.

◆ In a large sauté pan heat 3 tablespoons of the oil. Season the chicken lightly and brown it all over in the hot oil. Remove the chicken to a plate.

◆ Drain the sun-dried tomatoes and cut them into strips.

◆ Discard the fat in the pan and wipe it clean with kitchen paper. Pour in the remaining oil, add the onion and cook over a gentle heat until very soft, but don't let it brown or burn. Stir in the peppers, tomatoes, olives and, if using, the chilli flakes, then take the pan from the heat.

◆ Season to taste then spoon the mixture into a gratin or shallow freezer- and ovenproof dish. Arrange the chicken joints on the top.

TO FREEZE **Cover with foil or a double layer of cling film.**

TO DEFROST **Leave for 18–20 hours in the fridge or for 10–12 hours on the side. Make sure the chicken is completely defrosted before cooking.**

TO MICROWAVE **Follow your microwave instructions to defrost the chicken thoroughly and to cook it, adding the garlic as below.**

TO COOK **Finely chop 2 cloves of garlic. Remove the chicken breasts, sprinkle the garlic over the peppers then replace the breasts and brush them lightly with olive oil. Cover with foil and put in the oven at 160°C/325°F/gas 3 for 1–1 1/4 hours. Remove the foil for the last 20 minutes to let the chicken brown. Check that the chicken is thoroughly cooked before serving it.**

❄ LEMON CHICKEN WITH OLIVES AND OREGANO

This casserole must have its origins in Greece where olives abound and everything seems to be flavoured with oregano and is served either with whole lemons or plenty of the juice. Eaten bubbling hot from the oven it is a very refreshing casserole to serve al fresco on the sunniest of summer days. It is also cheering to eat it on a windy wet winter's day when memories of sun, sea and sand will all come flooding back.

SERVES 6

1 tablespoon olive oil

1.8–2kg/4–4½lb fresh free-range chicken, jointed into 6–8 pieces or 6 fresh free-range chicken joints.

20g/¾oz butter

1 onion, peeled and chopped

2 cloves garlic, peeled and chopped

1 unwaxed lemon, thinly sliced

50g/1¾oz black olives, stoned

2 teaspoons fresh oregano, chopped, or 1 teaspoon dried oregano

150ml/5fl oz dry white wine

600ml/1 pint chicken stock

Heat the oil in a sauté or frying pan large enough to hold all the chicken pieces. Season the chicken lightly and sauté in the oil, over a fairly high flame, until brown all over. Remove the pieces from the pan and drain off any excess fat.

◆ Lower the heat, add and melt the butter and cook the onion and garlic for a few minutes, taking care not to let them brown. When they are soft add the lemon and olives and cook for a further 2 minutes. Return the chicken to the pan, sprinkle on the oregano and pour in the wine. Bring to the boil and cook over a high heat until most of the liquid has evaporated. Add the stock, cover the pan and leave it to simmer for 10 minutes.

◆ Remove the chicken from the pan and leave the sauce to bubble until it has reduced by about a third. Take from the heat, remove and discard the pieces of lemon peel and check the seasoning.

TO FREEZE **Use a rigid freezer container or a freezer- and ovenproof casserole. Spoon in the sauce then pack the chicken pieces on the top and cover tightly.**

TO DEFROST **Leave on the side for 8–10 hours or in the fridge for up to 24 hours.**

TO MICROWAVE **Follow your microwave instructions to defrost the chicken thoroughly and, if you like, reheat and cook it.**

TO REHEAT **Preheat the oven to 160°C/325°F/gas 3 and cook the completely defrosted casserole for around 50 minutes to 1 hour or until the sauce is bubbling hot and the chicken is cooked.**

❄ CHICKEN IN SAFFRON AND ALMOND SAUCE

For me saffron always conjures up visions of the Middle East with great banquets of dark yellow-coloured food flecked with twinkling pieces of gold and silver leaf. However, to come down to earth, saffron is a wonderful spice with a fantastic colour and an elusive flavour and it certainly brings this dish to life. Don't be mean with it; when I say a good pinch that is what I mean.

   I have been deliberately vague about the amount of garam masala for two reasons: first, the powders all vary in strength; and second, some people might like a 'hot' sauce while others, especially if a good wine is being served, will only want a hint of curry.

SERVES 6

good pinch saffron threads

¼ teaspoon ground cinnamon

½–1 teaspoon garam masala powder

10–12 fresh free-range chicken thighs, skinned and boned

3 tablespoons oil

1 large onion, peeled and chopped

2 cloves garlic, peeled and finely chopped

2.5cm/1in piece ginger, finely chopped

100g/3½oz ground almonds

300ml/10fl oz chicken stock

50g/1¾oz raisins

Crumble the saffron threads and mix them with the cinnamon and garam masala. Cut the chicken into bite-sized pieces and sprinkle with the spices.

◆ Heat the oil in a large frying pan and sauté the onion, garlic and ginger until soft. Stir in the chicken, the ground almonds and the stock. Season, bring to the boil and let it simmer for 5 minutes. Take from the heat and stir in the raisins. Allow to cool completely.

TO FREEZE **Leave in the casserole or transfer to a rigid freezer container.**

TO DEFROST **Leave on the side for 8–10 hours or in the fridge for up to 24 hours.**

TO MICROWAVE **Follow your microwave instructions to defrost and cook the chicken casserole.**

TO COOK **Set the oven to 160°C/325°F/ gas 3 and cook the chicken for 1 hour.**

TO SERVE **Serve with plain boiled rice and follow it with a salad.**

❄ CHICKEN THIGHS WITH LIME AND HONEY

A friend and very good cook, Gisella Clanmorris, gave me the original idea for this recipe. The chicken thighs are marinated in honey and lime juice which is spiked with ginger and then just cooked before being frozen. After defrosting the thighs are bathed in the marinade then put into a very hot oven from which they emerge with a wonderful slightly burnt crispy skin that hides the sweet and succulent meat.

There is no need to be too accurate about the amount of honey: rather than weigh it out, it is much easier to pour in about half the jar - be fairly generous. Limes vary in size and juiciness and if you can only find small rather hard ones, use a couple more.

SERVES 6

12 fresh, free-range chicken thighs

3 large limes

225g/8oz or half a jar of runny honey

4cm/1½in piece ginger, peeled and chopped

Season the chicken thighs lightly. In a large bowl mix together the zest and juice of the limes, the honey and the ginger. Put in the chicken thighs and spoon the liquid all over them. Cover the bowl with a piece of cling film and refrigerate. Leave to marinate, turning the thighs occasionally, for at least 5 hours or, preferably, overnight.

◆ Transfer the thighs to a roasting tin. Pour over the marinade and cook in the oven at 180°C/350°F/gas 4 for 25-30 minutes. Leave until cool then remove the thighs from the tin and cut the bone out from each one and, using the skin, turn them into neat little parcels.

◆ Pour the marinade into a pan, bring to the boil and reduce it by about a third or until it has become slightly syrupy. Season it and leave to get cold.

TO FREEZE **Pack the thighs into a rigid freezer container and pour over the sauce.** TO DEFROST **Leave for for 6–7 hours on the side or 15–18 hours in the fridge.** TO MICROWAVE **Not suitable.** TO COOK **Put the thighs back into a roasting tin and spoon the sauce over the top. Preheat the oven to 220°C/425°F/gas 7 and cook for 20 minutes, basting the thighs with the sauce halfway through. Serve immediately.**

❄ COQ AU VIN

Properly made, coq au vin is one of the great dishes of the world but unfortunately it suffers, as do many classics, from being too well known and is frequently served up as a ghost of its proper self. The secret is simple: you need to use the very best quality ingredients and to cook it very slowly. It is always said that a coq au vin is better eaten as a reheated dish and as such it lends itself perfectly to freezing. That said, the mushrooms retain both their shape and bite better if they are added at the end. The chocolate is not discernible in the final sauce, but use it to add depth to the flavour.

In Alsace they make a lighter version using their local riesling instead of red wine, and very good it is too. This white wine version is basically the same but I would leave out the chocolate.

If everybody has a large appetite you can add to the chicken content by including a couple of extra chicken breasts with the bone in.

SERVES 6

2 tablespoons oil

1.8–2kg/4–4¹/₂lb fresh free-range chicken, jointed into 6 or 8 pieces or 6–8 fresh free-range chicken joints

100g/3¹/₂oz lardons

1 Spanish onion, peeled and chopped

50ml/2fl oz brandy

20g/³/₄oz flour

600ml/1 pint dry red wine

bouquet garni of parsley stalks, sprig thyme and bay leaf

25g/1oz bitter chocolate

about 300ml/10fl oz chicken stock

TO COOK

20g/³/₄oz butter

2 cloves garlic, peeled and chopped

250g/9oz button mushrooms, trimmed and sliced

Heat the oil in a large lidded sauté pan for preference; otherwise use a large ovenproof casserole.

◆ Sauté the chicken joints, in two batches if need be, until brown all over then remove them to a plate. Pour off most of the oil, add the bacon and onion and cook until the onion is soft. Return the chicken to the pan, warm the brandy, pour it over the chicken and very carefully set light to it. Shake the pan until all the flames have died down then sprinkle on the flour. Pour in the wine, add the herbs and chocolate, then pour in enough stock almost to cover the chicken joints and season.

◆ Cook for 30 minutes either on the hob at a very gentle simmer or in a low oven at 160°C/325°F/gas 3.

TO FREEZE **Discard the herbs then freeze in the casserole or transfer everything to rigid freezer containers.**

TO DEFROST **Leave on the side for 10–12 hours or in the fridge for 18–20 hours.**

TO MICROWAVE **Follow your microwave instructions to defrost the chicken and for the final reheating (see below).**

TO COOK **Remove the chicken to a plate and boil the sauce in the casserole until it has thickened and reduced by about a third. Return the chicken. Melt the butter in a frying pan, stir in the garlic, add the mushrooms and sauté them until soft. Stir them into the casserole. Reheat at a very gentle simmer or in a low oven, 160°C/325°F/gas 3, for 50 minutes.**

TO SERVE **It is nice and traditional to serve coq au vin on a meat dish with little triangles of fried bread arranged decoratively round the edge.**

COQ AU VIN WITH CARROTS
AND PEAS WITH SAGE (PAGE 126)

❄ CHICKEN IN THAI SAUCE

Thai food can be exceedingly hot and the first time I made this I was over-generous with the curry paste and nearly blew the roof off my mouth. I have tempered it considerably, especially as this book is about entertaining and you may well want to serve it with wine, but if you do all like it really hot you can always use more of the paste. It can be found in a red or green version in most supermarkets and either colour would be fine for this dish. Serve it with plain boiled rice, preferably fragrant Thai.

SERVES 6

700g/1lb 9oz fresh free-range chicken breasts, skinned and boned

2 shallots, peeled and roughly chopped

2 cloves garlic, peeled and chopped

2.5cm/1in piece ginger, peeled and roughly chopped

zest 1 lime

2 stalks lemon grass, split in half

$\frac{1}{2}$ teaspoon turmeric

2 teaspoons Thai curry paste

400ml/14fl oz can coconut milk

1 teaspoon cornflour

150g/5$\frac{1}{2}$oz thick plain yoghurt

Cut the chicken breasts into bite-sized pieces and reserve.

◆ Put everything, except the cornflour and yoghurt, into a pan, bring to the boil and simmer gently for 30 minutes. Pour the sauce through a sieve, return it to the cleaned-out pan and season. Slake the cornflour in 3 tablespoons of water and stir it into the sauce together with the yoghurt then the reserved chicken pieces. Stirring constantly, bring to the boil and simmer for 2–3 minutes, adding, if needed, a little more water.

◆ Take the pan from the heat, adjust the seasoning and set aside until cold.

TO FREEZE **Transfer to a freezer- and ovenproof casserole or rigid freezer container.**

TO DEFROST **Leave on the side for 7–8 hours or in the fridge for 16–18 hours.**

TO MICROWAVE **Follow your microwave instructions to defrost and cook the chicken.**

TO COOK **Put the chicken with its sauce in a covered casserole into the oven at 160°C/325°F/gas 3 for 1 hour.**

❄ CHICKEN BREASTS AND ARTICHOKE PARCELS

A lovely dish for a party that has the bonus of being very quick and easy to make.

Jars of artichoke sauce or paste can be found on the supermarket shelves, but you could use a can of artichoke hearts and drain them before whizzing them to a paste in a food processor with some olive oil, a few capers, a spoonful of vinegar and seasoning. If you have easy access to fresh artichokes you could use the hearts to make a sensational dish.

SERVES 6

680g/1lb 8oz packet puff pastry

125g/4¹/₂oz butter

6 fresh free-range chicken breasts, skinned and boned

250g/9oz artichoke sauce or paste

Fully defrost the puff pastry and roll it out very thinly. Cut the sheets into 6 equal rectangles.

◆ Melt the butter. Holding a chicken breast, good side down, spoon some artichoke purée onto it, then place it on a piece of the pastry. Generously brush the top of the chicken with butter and bring up the sides of the pastry to meet in the middle. Pinch neatly together to seal the pastry at both ends and give a tidy-looking parcel. Repeat with the remaining chicken breasts.

TO FREEZE **Wrap in plastic freezer bags.**
TO DEFROST **Leave in the fridge for 18–24 hours.**
TO MICROWAVE **Not suitable.**
TO COOK **Bake at 200°C/400°F/gas 6 for 35–40 minutes, by which time the chicken will be cooked and the pastry beautifully golden. You may find that you need to cover the pastry for the last 10 minutes in order to stop it burning at the edges. Serve direct from the oven.**

❄ CREAMY CHICKEN AND VEGETABLE PIE

A pie covered with golden brown, beautifully risen puff pastry is always a welcome sight. This one, made with chicken thighs and vegetables in a wine and cream sauce flavoured with mustard and parsley, always goes down well. It also is excellent for the freezer and the chicken emerges from under the crust perfectly cooked and beautifully tender.

SERVES 6

10–12 fresh free-range chicken thighs, skinned and boned

4 tablespoons oil

25g/1oz butter

4 leeks, white part only, sliced

4–5 celery sticks, sliced

200g/7oz baby carrots, sliced

2 tablespoons flour

150ml/5fl oz white wine

200ml/7fl oz whipping cream

good bunch parsley, chopped

1 teaspoon Dijon mustard

350g/12oz sheet puff pastry

Cut each chicken thigh into 2-3 pieces. If the pastry is frozen put it out to defrost.

◆ Heat a couple of tablespoons of the oil and the butter in a pan, add the vegetables and gently fry them for 2-3 minutes before adding 200ml/7fl oz of water and some salt and pepper. Cover the pan and leave the vegetables to stew for a further 5 minutes or until soft. Strain off and reserve the cooking liquid and put the vegetables into a deep pie dish.

◆ Heat the remaining oil in a sauté or large frying pan and sauté the chicken pieces until lightly browned. Remove them to a plate covered with kitchen paper, pat the oil off the skin with more paper. Add the chicken pieces to the vegetables in the pie dish and stir to mix them together.

◆ Pour off any excess oil from the pan, stir in the flour, then pour in the reserved liquid from the vegetables and the wine. Bring to the boil and, stirring constantly, let it simmer for 2-3 minutes. Take it from the heat and add the cream, parsley and mustard and season to taste, then pour it into the pie dish.

◆ Roll out the pastry to a size bigger than the pie dish then cut off the corners and roll them into strips. Lay the strips round the edge of the pie dish, brush them with cold water then lay the pastry cover on the top. Trim off the excess, then press down the edges with fingers or a knife and finally knock up the pastry round the outside edge with a knife.

TO FREEZE **Cover with foil or a double layer of cling film.**

TO DEFROST **Leave on the side for 7–9 hours or for up to 24 hours in the fridge.**

TO MICROWAVE **Not suitable.**

TO COOK **Uncover and put in an oven pre-heated to 220°C/425°F/gas 7 for 20 minutes then reduce the temperature to180°C/ 350°F/gas 4 and cook for a further 30 minutes.**

❄ GUINEA FOWL WITH YOGHURT, LIME AND CORIANDER

Guinea fowl are lovely tasting birds but they do have a tendency to be a little dry and slightly tough. This way of cooking them overcomes both problems and you finish up with a sharpish but meltingly delicious sauce. You may have a friendly butcher who will joint the birds for you, but it isn't difficult to remove the legs and breasts. There is no worthwhile meat on the wings so boil them up with the carcass to make a decent stock which can then be used instead of chicken stock in any of the soup recipes.

After many experiments I have decided that it is nicest to smother the joints in the marinade and then immediately freeze them. Then, to give the marinade a chance to work, I slowly defrost the dish in the fridge and finally cook the casserole for a long time in a low oven.

As the guinea fowl is cooked in the marinade the yoghurt needs to be stabilised which is done by stirring in some cornflour. Don't leave this stage out, or the yoghurt will curdle and the sauce will separate. Use a good quality yoghurt. I like to use the bio ones which have a good consistency and a nice taste.

SERVES 6–8

2 fresh guinea fowl

2 level tablespoons cornflour

350g/12oz plain yoghurt

3 cloves garlic, peeled and finely sliced

2.5cm/1in piece ginger, peeled and finely sliced

1 teaspoon chilli flakes

zest 1 and juice 2 limes

3 tablespoons oil

TO FINISH
bunch coriander, chopped

Start by jointing the birds. Pull out one leg of the bird and, using a sharp knife, gradually cut it away from the carcass and finally remove the leg by cutting through the joint.

◆ Pull off the skin and cut off and discard the end of the leg. Do the same with the other leg. With a sharp pointed knife cut one side of the breast from the breast bone and follow round, cutting it away from the wishbone until the breast comes away from the bird. Do the same with the other breast. Skin both breasts. Repeat with the other bird.

◆ Stir the cornflour into 2 tablespoons of water and mix it into the yoghurt then stir in the garlic, ginger, chilli flakes, zest and juice of the limes and the oil. Season.

◆ Put the guinea fowl joints into a dish or casserole large enough to hold them then spoon the marinade over them and turn them so that they are well covered.

TO FREEZE Cover the dish or casserole with foil or a double layer of cling film.

TO DEFROST Leave for at least 24 hours in the fridge.

TO MICROWAVE I think this dish takes up the flavours better if it is cooked conventionally but you could, following the instructions for your oven, defrost and cook the casserole in a microwave then finish as below.

TO COOK Make sure the casserole is completely defrosted. Heat the oven to 160°C/325°F/gas 3. Stir the sauce then put the casserole into the oven and cook for 2 hours. Take it out a couple of times to stir the sauce and turn the joints.

TO FINISH Remove the joints to a serving dish then adjust the seasoning and stir the sauce well. Pour the sauce over the guinea fowl and sprinkle the coriander on top.

❄ DUCK BREASTS IN HONEY AND GRAPEFRUIT SAUCE

Ready-prepared duck breasts are a boon for the cook as they need very little preparation and are enhanced by many different flavours. This recipe uses a simple sweet and sour sauce into which the lightly cooked breasts are immersed just before freezing. I defrost the dish some time ahead and then turn the breasts in the marinade and leave the dish in the fridge for several hours longer before cooking.

I make it with the breasts of the normal farmhouse duck but you could use the large ones from a Barbary duck, when 4 should suffice for 6 people.

SERVES 6

4–6 fresh duck breasts, depending on size

5 tablespoons runny honey

juice 1 pink grapefruit

2 tablespoons wine vinegar

1 tablespoon soy sauce

2.5cm/1in piece ginger, peeled and finely chopped

TO FINISH

50g/1³/₄oz very cold butter

bunch coriander, chopped

Use a fork to prick the fat on the breasts then put them, fat side down, in a frying pan. Cook over a low to medium heat for 5–8 minutes or until most of the fat has run out.

◆ Take the breasts from the pan and wipe off any remaining fat by patting them all over with kitchen paper then put them in a shallow freezer- and ovenproof dish.

◆ Combine the honey, grapefruit juice, vinegar, soy sauce and ginger and pour it over the duck.

TO FREEZE **Cover with foil or a double layer of cling film.**

TO DEFROST **Leave on the side for 6–7 hours, turn the breasts in the marinade, then leave in the fridge for a few hours longer. Or leave in the fridge for at least 24 hours for the dish to defrost and soak up the marinade.**

TO MICROWAVE **Follow the instructions for your microwave to defrost and cook the duck. Then finish as below.**

TO COOK **Season the breasts and put the covered dish in the oven heated to 160°C/325°F/gas 3 for 40–45 minutes or until they are just cooked, but still pink in the centre.**

TO FINISH **Pour the juices into a pan and keep the breasts warm in a very low oven. Boil down the juices, stirring constantly as they will catch and burn very easily. Finally whisk in the butter and season to taste. Cut the duck breasts into slices then pour the sauce over them, sprinkle with coriander and serve immediately.**

❄ DUCK CASSEROLE WITH OLIVES

Another Provençal combination and one that comes in many different forms. For this version I have used black olives and red wine - try to use a strong one of the type found in Provence such as Bandol.

I make up the bouquet garni myself using a swivel potato peeler to peel the orange and wrapping the pieces round the herbs before tying it all together.

SERVES 6

4–6 fresh duck breasts, depending on size

2 onions, peeled and sliced

40g/1¹/₂oz flour

300ml/10fl oz red wine

200ml/7fl oz duck or chicken stock

juice 1 orange

2 tablespoons tomato purée

bouquet garni of parsley stalks, bay leaf, sprig thyme and peel ¹/₂ orange

TO REHEAT

100g/3¹/₂oz black olives, pitted

1–3 cloves garlic, peeled and very finely chopped

Heat a large frying pan and fry the duck breasts, skin side down, over a medium heat, for 5-7 minutes to release the fat. Turn them over and fry for just 1-2 minutes to brown the meat. Remove the breasts to a large plate lined with a double layer of kitchen paper and use more paper to blot the fat from the breasts.

◆ Pour off all but 2 tablespoons of fat from the pan then add the onions and cook over a low heat until soft. Stir in the flour, then add the wine, stock, orange juice, tomato purée and the bouquet garni and, stirring constantly, bring the sauce to the boil. Season with pepper and just a smidgin of salt and leave to simmer for a few minutes, then remove from the heat and allow to cool.

TO FREEZE **Pack the duck into rigid freezer containers or a freezer- and oven-proof casserole and pour over the sauce. Seal and freeze.**

TO DEFROST **Leave on the side for 8–10 hours or in the fridge for 18–20 hours.**

TO MICROWAVE **Follow the instructions for your microwave to defrost. Add the olives and garlic. Reheat, then finish as below.**

TO REHEAT **If you froze the duck in a container transfer it and the sauce to a casserole. Stir in the olives and garlic and cook in a low oven, 160°C/325°F/gas 3, for 1¹/₄ hours.**

TO FINISH **Remove the bouquet garni. Take the breasts from the casserole, cut them into slices and serve covered with the warm sauce.**

❄ DUCK BREASTS WITH MANGO SAUCE

This is really duck gone Thai. The breasts are marinated in lime juice with some lemon grass and then briefly roasted, to remove most of their fat. They are then frozen together with the piquant mango sauce and, after defrosting, slowly cooked in the oven.

As for the recipe on page 72 I make this dish with the breasts of the normal farmhouse duck but you could use the large ones from a Barbary duck in which case 4 should feed 6 people.

SERVES 6

1 stick lemon grass

1½ limes

4 tablespoons oil

4–6 fresh duck breasts, depending on size

2 shallots

2 cloves garlic

2.5cm/1in piece ginger

pinch chilli flakes

½ teaspoon turmeric

1 very large or 2 smaller not too ripe mango

Remove the outer peel from the lemon grass, and put it, along with the zest and juice of 1 lime and 2 tablespoons of oil, into a large shallow ovenproof dish. Put the duck breasts, skin side up, into this and leave them to marinate for 4-5 hours.

◆ Heat the oven to 190°C/375°F/gas 5, put in the dish with the duck breasts and cook for 20 minutes. Take from the oven and put the breasts on a plate and pat with kitchen paper to remove the fat. Discard the lemon grass, pour the liquid into a gravy jug or similar and allow the fat to rise.

◆ Peel and chop the shallots and garlic and cook them gently in the remaining oil. When softened stir in the peeled and chopped ginger, the chopped centre stalk of the lemon grass, the chilli flakes, turmeric and zest and juice of the remaining half lime. Pour off as much fat as you can from the cooling marinade, add the juices to the sauce and season to taste. Stir everything together then take the pan from the heat. Peel, destone the mango, cube the flesh and stir into the sauce.

TO FREEZE **Use a shallow freezer- and ovenproof dish. Spread the sauce over the bottom of the dish and put the duck breasts, skin side up, on top. Cover with foil or a double layer of cling film.**

TO DEFROST **Leave on the side for 6–8 hours or for 15–18 hours in the fridge.**

TO MICROWAVE **Not suitable.**

TO COOK **Cook at 160°C/325°F/gas 3 for 40–45 minutes. The breasts still want to be slightly pink in the centre. If you have a grill in the top of your oven turn it on a few minutes before the end of the cooking time to crisp up the skin.**

TO FINISH **The duck needs to be served straight from the dish. If you have used Barbary duck you will need to slice the breasts before serving.**

TO SERVE **I like to serve it with rice flavoured with shallots and turmeric. Green vegetables or a root vegetable purée such as Carrot and Parsnip Ripple (page 121) also go well.**

❄ POT ROASTED PHEASANT WITH ORANGE AND CHESTNUT SAUCE

Chestnuts have a great affinity with pheasant, and this sauce, flavoured with orange and thickened with chestnut purée, is very easy and also one of the best ways of cooking birds after Christmas when they could be on the old side. Small cans of chestnut purée don't seem to exist but any left over can be frozen and used for a pudding.

SERVES 6–8

25g/1oz butter

1 tablespoon oil

150g/5¹/₂oz unsmoked streaky bacon, roughly chopped

3 shallots, peeled and roughly chopped

brace of pheasants

2 tablespoons brandy

1 tablespoon flour

150ml/5fl oz red wine

150ml/5fl oz pheasant, chicken or vegetable stock

zest and juice 1 large orange

425g/15oz can unsweetened chestnut purée

Set the oven to heat to 160°C/325°F/gas 3.

◆ In a heavy casserole, large enough to take both the birds, heat the butter and oil, add the bacon and cook over a medium heat until the fat runs. Stir in the shallots and cook until they have softened. Use a slotted spoon to scoop out the bacon and shallots and keep them on one side. Raise the heat and brown the birds all over. Warm the brandy, pour it over the birds and carefully set light to it. Rotate and shake the casserole until the flames die down.

◆ Remove the birds from the casserole, put them onto a plate and sprinkle them with well-seasoned flour. Return the shallots and bacon to the casserole and place the birds, breast down, on top. Pour in the wine and stock, season lightly and cover the casserole tightly. Put into the hot oven and cook for 1 hour, turning the birds every 15 minutes.

◆ Remove the birds from the casserole and return it to the hob. Stir the orange zest and juice and the chestnut purée into the sauce, bring it to the boil and simmer for 5-10 minutes or until it has thickened and has a good texture. Leave to cool.

◆ Cut each bird into four joints or carve into smaller pieces and put into the casserole. Spoon the sauce over them and leave on the side until everything is cold.

TO FREEZE **If the casserole will fit into your freezer, first cover it tightly. Otherwise pack the joints and sauce into a rigid freezer container or containers.**

TO DEFROST **Leave on the side for 8–10 hours or in the fridge for 18 hours. Make sure the pheasant is fully defrosted before cooking it.**

TO MICROWAVE **Follow the instructions for your microwave to defrost the casserole thoroughly. Reheat on full power to ensure the pheasant is completely cooked.**

TO REHEAT **If you used plastic boxes return the pheasant and the sauce to a casserole and cover with a lid. Heat the oven to 160°C/325°F/gas 3 and cook for 30–40 minutes or until the casserole is hot through. Check the seasoning and serve.**

❄ PHEASANT BREASTS IN SPICY LEEK SAUCE

A friend, Susie Hilleary, who cooks game and fish to perfection, was generous enough to give me one of her recipes on which this is based.

If you are short of time you can sometimes find pheasant breasts in the supermarket but it is far more satisfactory to use whole pheasants. Cut off the breasts and use them for this dish, then cut off the legs and use them in a casserole. Alternatively, you could use the legs in the Pheasant Crumble on page 78 or you could mix them with other game for the Game Cobbler on page 82. You can then use the carcasses to make a lovely rich stock, which you could use for this dish or keep in the freezer for another occasion.

The addition of garam masala is optional but a little, just enough to give the sauce a slightly nutty taste, is very good.

SERVES 6

2–3 leeks

3 sticks celery

50g/1³⁄₄oz butter

2 tablespoons oil

6 pheasant breasts

2 tablespoons brandy

1 large onion, peeled and finely chopped

1–2 teaspoons garam masala powder or paste

25g/1oz flour

200ml/7fl oz pheasant or chicken stock

200ml/7fl oz double cream

Wash the leeks, discard any dark green parts, then split them into half. Cut each half lengthwise into four or five then cut the strips into lengths of around 2.5cm/1in. Strip any stringy bits from the celery and then chop it.

◆ Heat the butter and oil in a large pan and quickly brown the pheasant breasts on both sides. Warm the brandy, pour it over the pheasant, set light to it and shake the pan until the flames die down. Remove the breasts to a plate, turn down the heat, add the onion to the pan and sauté until soft and light golden in colour. Add the leeks and celery, turn the heat up slightly and cook for 2 minutes or so before stirring in the garam masala then the flour. Cook for a minute then pour in the stock followed by the cream. Season, bring the sauce slowly to the boil, and then let it bubble gently for 3-4 minutes.

◆ Remove from the heat and leave to cool.

TO FREEZE **Put the pheasant breasts into a freezer-and ovenproof gratin dish and pour over the sauce. Cover with foil.**
TO DEFROST **Leave on the side for 6–7 hours or in the fridge for at least 15 hours.**
TO MICROWAVE **Follow the instructions for your microwave to defrost and cook the chicken breasts.**
TO COOK **Heat the oven to 160°C/ 325°F/gas 3. Cook the covered dish for 1¹⁄₄ hours.**

❄ PHEASANT CRUMBLE

Another friend, Erica Austen, told me that she constantly makes pheasant crumble as it is her husband's favourite way of eating the bird. I immediately cottoned onto the idea and here is my version of her recipe, written especially for the freezer. It is fast becoming my husband's favourite way of eating pheasant!

SERVES 8

juice 1 orange (and zest for crumble)

50g/1³/₄oz raisins

50g/1³/₄oz butter

1 tablespoon oil

brace of pheasants

200g/7oz lardons or roughly chopped streaky bacon

2 large onions, peeled and roughly chopped

2 large carrots, peeled and roughly chopped

2 sticks celery, strings removed and chopped

3 tablespoons brandy

250ml/9fl oz dry cider

300ml/10fl oz pheasant or chicken stock

bouquet garni of parsley stalks, sprigs thyme and bay leaf

2 tablespoons cornflour

1 tablespoon redcurrant jelly

FOR THE CRUMBLE

125g/4¹/₂oz flour

50g/1³/₄oz porridge oats

50g/1³/₄oz flaked almonds

zest 1 orange

125g/4¹/₂oz butter

Zest and juice the orange. Reserve the zest for the crumble and put the raisins to soak in the juice.

◆ Heat the butter and oil in a large casserole or pan and gently sauté the birds, turning from time to time, until they are golden on all sides. Remove and keep them on one side. Fry the bacon until the fat has run then remove with a slotted spoon and reserve.

◆ Sauté the onions, carrots and celery until the onion is soft and golden then return the pheasants, breast uppermost, and the bacon. In a small pan warm the brandy, set light to it, pour it over the pheasants and shake the pan until the flames have died down. Add the cider, chicken stock, the raisins and any remaining orange juice and the bouquet garni. Season then bring to the boil. Cover the pan and either put it in the oven at 160°C/325°F/gas 3 or simmer on the hob for 40 minutes to 1 hour or until the pheasants are just cooked. (The time needed depends on the age and size of the pheasants.)

◆ Meanwhile make the crumble. In a bowl mix together the flour, porridge oats, almonds, orange zest and some salt and pepper. Add the butter, chopped into small pieces and rub it in, as if you were making pastry, until you reach the crumb stage. Keep until needed.

◆ Take the cooked pheasants from the pan and leave to cool. Mix the cornflour with 3 tablespoons of the juices, pour it back into the pan then bring the sauce to the boil and stir until thickened. Add redcurrant jelly to taste and check the seasoning.

◆ Bone the pheasants and cut the meat into bite-sized pieces. Stir the meat into the sauce then transfer everything to a clean casserole or large gratin dish. Leave until cold then sprinkle the crumble over the top.

TO FREEZE **Cover with foil or a double layer of cling film.**

TO DEFROST **Leave on the side for 10–12 hours or in the fridge for 24 hours.**

TO MICROWAVE **Not suitable.**

TO REHEAT **Bake in the oven at 180°C/350°F/gas 4 for 30–40 minutes or until everything is hot and the crumble golden. The casserole can then be held in a low oven for up to 1 hour.**

PHEASANT CRUMBLE WITH PIQUANT RED CABBAGE

(PAGE 124)

❄ PIGEON BREASTS IN MARSALA SAUCE

Pigeon has a wonderful rich gamey taste and this sauce made with marsala and stock from the carcasses sets it off beautifully. The legs and wings of pigeons are minuscule and really bony so the only parts really worth eating are the breasts. You will need to cut them from the birds, which is not difficult, or perhaps you could ask a friendly butcher. Before you prepare the casserole, allow time to make a rich stock from the carcasses.

I find the amounts rather a problem. Hungry people will eat 2 breasts each and others just 1. I am inclined, for 6 people, to buy 4-5 pigeons giving 8-10 breasts.

SERVES 6

4 or 5 pigeons

1 small onion, peeled and roughly chopped

1 carrot, peeled and roughly chopped

1 stick celery, roughly chopped

4 peppercorns

75g/2³⁄₄oz raisins

100ml/3¹⁄₂fl oz marsala wine

200g/7oz chestnut mushrooms

250g/9oz baby onions

4 tablespoons oil

125g/4¹⁄₂oz rindless streaky bacon, chopped

50g/1³⁄₄oz butter

3 tablespoons flour

TO FINISH (optional)

25g/1oz butter

25g/1oz flour

Use a boning or sharply pointed knife to cut down the centre of the breastbone of each pigeon and scrape down the side to loosen the breast and then cut it off the body. Repeat with the other breast and the other birds. Keep the breasts refrigerated in a covered dish.

◆ Put the carcasses into a large pan with the onion, carrot, celery and peppercorns and cover everything with water. Bring to the boil, skim thoroughly then cover the pan and leave it to simmer for 2 hours. Strain the stock into a clean pan, bring it to the boil and let it bubble hard for around 20 minutes or until the stock has reduced by about half and concentrated in flavour. Keep it on one side.

◆ Meanwhile put the raisins to soak in the marsala. Destalk and peel the mushrooms then cut them into thick slices.

◆ Immerse the onions in boiling water for 2 minutes. Drain, cool slightly, and the skins will slip off easily.

◆ Heat 3 tablespoons of the oil in a large sauté or frying pan, add the bacon, cook until all the fat has run, then remove it to a plate with a slotted spoon. Add the onions, turn up the heat a little and cook until they are speckled with brown then remove them to a plate.

◆ Throw out the fat and wipe the pan clean with kitchen paper. Melt half the butter, add the mushrooms and toss and turn them for a couple of minutes or until they have soaked up the fat and are browning on the outside. Remove them to a plate.

◆ Dry the pigeon breasts with kitchen paper and then roll them in seasoned flour. In a large, clean pan heat the remaining butter and oil and quickly brown the breasts on both sides. Add the marsala and raisins, 300ml/10fl oz of the stock, the bacon, onions and mushrooms and seasoning to taste. Bring to the boil and let it simmer for 10 minutes before taking it from the hob and leave it to cool.

TO FREEZE **Transfer to a freezer- and ovenproof casserole or to a rigid freezer container.**

TO DEFROST **Leave on the side for 8–10 hours or in the fridge for 16–18 hours.**

TO MICROWAVE **Follow the instructions for your microwave to defrost and cook.**

TO COOK **Cook the defrosted casserole in the oven at 160°C/325°F/gas 3 for 1¹⁄₂ hours. It will come to no harm if it is left for 2 hours.**

TO FINISH **If you like a thicker sauce you can finish it off by putting the casserole on the hob and stirring in a spoonful of beurre manié (equal quantities of butter and flour mashed together).**

❄ RABBIT IN CIDER WITH HERBS AND DIJON MUSTARD

Sadly, rabbit seldom features on the British table. Perhaps this is a legacy from the war when rabbit was easily available, but the other ingredients needed to make a good casserole were non-existent, so by default rabbit gained a reputation for being pretty nasty. The French have always enjoyed rabbit and this recipe with cider, herbs and mustard is one of their favourite ways of cooking it.

SERVES 6

300ml/10fl oz strong dry cider

few parsley stalks

6 juniper berries, lightly crushed

2 sage leaves

bunch thyme

6 large rabbit joints, rinsed under cold water and wiped dry

3 tablespoons flour

½ teaspoon English mustard powder

25g/1oz butter

2 tablespoons oil

1 large onion, peeled and chopped

2 tablespoons brandy

300ml/10fl oz light chicken stock

2 cloves garlic, peeled and crushed

1 tablespoon Dijon mustard

Pour the cider into a bowl, add the parsley stalks, lightly crushed juniper berries, sage leaves, half the thyme and immerse the rabbit in it. Leave 4-5 hours, turning the rabbit once or twice.

◆ Take the rabbit from the marinade and pat dry with kitchen paper. Season the flour with salt and pepper, add the mustard powder to it and put it into a plastic bag. Add the rabbit and shake the bag to coat the rabbit with flour.

◆ In a large sauté or frying pan heat the butter and oil and sauté the onion until soft. Remove the onion from the pan with a slotted spoon and brown the rabbit joints. Warm the brandy, pour it over the rabbit and immediately set light to it. Shake the pan until the flames have all died down then return the onion. Strain the marinade and add, together with the stock. Stir in the garlic, the Dijon mustard and remaining thyme and bring to the boil. Let it simmer for 10 minutes then remove from the heat and leave until cold.

TO FREEZE **Turn into a freezer- and oven-proof casserole dish or a rigid freezer container.**

TO DEFROST **Leave on the side for 8–10 hours or in the fridge for up to 24 hours.**

TO MICROWAVE **Follow your microwave instructions to defrost and cook the casserole, then finish as below.**

TO COOK **Cook in the oven at 160°C/325°F/gas 3 for 1¼ hours.**

TO FINISH **Before serving taste the sauce and, if necessary, stir in a little more Dijon mustard and salt and pepper.**

❄ GAME COBBLER

The culinary definition of a cobbler is a fruit pie with a scone topping. Here fruit is replaced by game but I feel it is still legitimate to call it cobbler; it somehow conjures up homely and comfortable feelings.

From October through to the spring, many supermarkets sell packets of mixed game for a casserole which I find very useful and have taken to using quite a lot. If you prefer, you could make the cobbler using all venison. The chocolate adds to the intensity of flavours.

Reheating the pie covered with damp greaseproof paper may be old-fashioned but it not only keeps the scones beautifully moist, it also allows the heat to penetrate the pie so that it heats up very evenly.

SERVES 6

900g–1kg/2lb–2lb 4oz mixed game or venison

2 tablespoons flour

2 tablespoons oil

1 onion, peeled and chopped

2 cloves garlic, peeled and chopped

125g/4¹/₂oz unsmoked streaky bacon, chopped

400ml/14fl oz light game or chicken stock or water

50ml/2fl oz red wine

1 tablespoon tomato purée

1 tablespoon fresh marjoram, chopped, or 1 teaspoon dried marjoram

25g/1oz bitter chocolate

2 tablespoons redcurrant jelly

4 juniper berries, crushed

FOR THE TOPPING

350g/12oz self-raising flour

1 teaspoon baking powder

1 tablespoon parsley, chopped

1 teaspoon fresh marjoram, chopped, or ¹/₂ teaspoon dried marjoram

60g/2¹/₄oz cold butter

1 egg

200ml/7fl oz buttermilk or milk

Cube the game, discarding any gristle or membrane.

◆ Put the flour and some salt and pepper into a plastic bag, add the game and shake to cover it well with the flour.

◆ Heat the oil, sauté the onion and garlic until soft and, using a slotted spoon, remove them from the pan. Add the bacon and when it has released its fat turn up the heat and stir in the game. Quickly brown it all over then add all the remaining ingredients. Bring to the boil and either leave it to simmer, stirring occasionally, on the hob for 1 hour or transfer it to the oven preheated to 180°C/350°F/gas 4 and cook for 1 hour.

◆ When the casserole is cooked transfer the game to a pie dish or similar; a lasagne dish would be suitable. Don't worry if there is a lot of liquid as the base of the scones will soak it up. Heat the oven to 220°C/425°F/gas 7.

◆ Make the scones for the topping either by hand or by combining the flour, baking powder, herbs, ¹/₂ teaspoon salt and a good grinding of pepper in a food processor and quickly whizzing them together. Cube the butter and add it to the herb mixture and continue processing until you have fine crumbs. In a small bowl, whisk the egg and add half of it to the milk and then, with the machine running, pour it in through the feed tube. Stop the machine the moment the dough has amalgamated.

◆ Working quickly, turn the dough into a ball and use your fingers to pat it out to 1¹/₂cm/¹/₂in thick. Cut the scones into rounds with a 6cm/2¹/₂in cutter and arrange them, slightly overlapping, on top of the pie dish. Mix a little salt into the remaining egg and brush it over the top of the scones. Bake immediately for 12-15 minutes or until the scones have risen and are golden or the scones will become tough.

TO FREEZE Leave the cobbler until it is completely cold then wrap well in foil or a plastic bag before freezing.

TO DEFROST Leave for 8–10 hours on the side or for up to 24 hours in the fridge.

TO MICROWAVE Not suitable.

TO REHEAT Heat the oven to 190°C/375°F/gas 5. Cover the pie with a double layer of dampened greaseproof paper or foil and heat for 30–40 minutes. Remove the paper for the last 10 minutes to let the scones turn a good dark golden brown.

meat

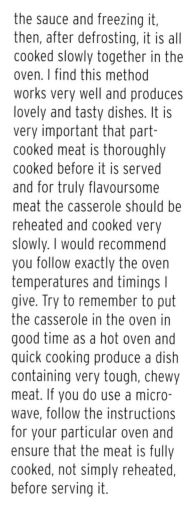

Many recipes in this chapter are casseroles or meat or ham in a sauce. Casseroles especially are perfect for the freezer as, more often than not, they are better for being made a day ahead and then the following day slowly cooked to give the sauce and the meat a chance to marry. In most recipes I have only browned or lightly cooked the meat before adding it to the sauce and freezing it, then, after defrosting, it is all cooked slowly together in the oven. I find this method works very well and produces lovely and tasty dishes. It is very important that part-cooked meat is thoroughly cooked before it is served and for truly flavoursome meat the casserole should be reheated and cooked very slowly. I would recommend you follow exactly the oven temperatures and timings I give. Try to remember to put the casserole in the oven in good time as a hot oven and quick cooking produce a dish containing very tough, chewy meat. If you do use a micro-wave, follow the instructions for your particular oven and ensure that the meat is fully cooked, not simply reheated, before serving it.

❄ NAVARIN OF LAMB

The classic French navarin often has the word *printanier* added to its name which simply means that the best navarins are made in the spring with young vegetables and the tender new season's lamb. If you grow your own or have access to really fresh vegetables and young home-reared lamb you could make a really sensational Whitsun casserole. That said, I made one in the autumn using rather older, but still British, lamb and really fresh, if large, root vegetables together with imported beans and frozen peas: it totally lived up to my expectations.

I have made navarins with various cuts of lamb and have decided that shoulder, which has some of the sweetest meat, is the nicest. The weight of the boned joint might sound a lot but you do need to cut off and discard most of the fat before cubing the meat and cooking the navarin.

SERVES 6

1.3–1.5kg/3lb–3lb 5oz fresh boned shoulder of lamb

250g/9oz carrots

125g/4½oz young turnips

150g/5½oz baby white onions or pickling onions, trimmed

2 tablespoons oil

½ Spanish onion, peeled and chopped

2 tablespoons granulated sugar

3 tablespoons flour

250ml/9fl oz dry white wine

300ml/10fl oz light lamb or vegetable stock or water

2 tablespoons tomato purée

2 cloves garlic, peeled and chopped

bouquet garni of parsley stalks, sprig thyme and bay leaf

TO FINISH

100g/3½oz shelled fresh peas or frozen petits pois

100g/3½oz fine French beans

Cut off and discard any surplus fat from the lamb then cut the meat into 2.5cm/1in cubes. Peel the carrots and turnips and cut them into chunks. If you feel professional you can then trim off the edges and turn each chunk into a lozenge shape; the finished result does look very good. Bring a small pan of water to the boil, cook the pickling onions for 1 minute then drain and peel them.

◆ Set the oven to heat to 180°C/350°/gas 4. Heat the oil in a large frying pan and gently sauté the Spanish onion until transparent. Turn up the heat high then add the lamb and sprinkle over the sugar. Stir constantly until the meat has browned all over then reduce the heat again and sprinkle on the flour. Continue stirring for 1 minute then transfer the meat and onion to a casserole that can be used on the hob. Use the wine to deglaze the pan, scraping up any juicy pieces that may have stuck to the bottom, and pour everything over the meat. Add the stock or water to the casserole with the tomato purée, garlic, bouquet garni and some seasoning and finally stir in the prepared vegetables. Put the casserole into the hot oven and cook for 45 minutes.

◆ Take the casserole from the oven and use a slotted spoon to remove the meat and vegetables to a bowl. Return the casserole to the hob, bring it to the boil and let it bubble for 5-10 minutes to let the flavours concentrate and the gravy reduce and thicken. Take the casserole from the hob, check the seasoning and return the meat and vegetables.

TO FREEZE Leave until cold before covering and freezing, either in the casserole, if suitable, or in a rigid freezer container.

TO DEFROST Leave on the side for 8–9 hours or for at least 20 hours in the fridge. Discard any fat that has settled on the top.

TO MICROWAVE Follow the instructions for your oven to defrost and reheat.

TO REHEAT Heat the oven to 160°C/ 325°F/gas 3 and cook the casserole for 1½–2 hours. If the casserole was not completely defrosted cook for a little longer.

TO FINISH Just before serving the navarin, cook the fresh peas, if using, for a few minutes until just tender. Top and tail the beans and in a separate pan cook them until just tender and, if using frozen petits pois, add them to this pan for the last 30 seconds. Take the hot casserole from the oven and stir in the peas and beans.

CASSEROLE OF LOIN CHOPS AND CANNELLINI BEANS

In France beans are often served alongside lamb and a very good combination they are too. If you feel energetic you could buy a packet of dried beans and soak and cook them but I find the other flavours in this dish are so strong that tinned beans work very well. I particularly like cannellini beans but you could always use tinned haricots or flageolets.

The chops are quite bulky so if you freeze the dish in a casserole you will need a large one and space in your freezer.

SERVES 6

12 fresh lamb loin chops

2 x 400g/14oz cans cannellini beans

2 onions, peeled and chopped

2–3 cloves garlic, peeled and chopped

3 tablespoons olive oil

2 x 400g/14oz cans chopped tomatoes

2 tablespoons tomato purée

150ml/5fl.oz red wine

bouquet garni of parsley stalks, sprig thyme and bay leaf or 2 sachets bouquet garni

Trim the chops of any excess fat and set on one side.

◆ Rinse the beans well under running water, drain and reserve.

◆ Use a large frying pan to cook the onions and garlic gently in the oil until soft. Use a slotted spoon to remove them from the pan, then turn up the heat and quickly brown the chops on both sides. Remove the chops then return the onion and garlic to the pan and add the tomatoes, tomato purée, wine and bouquet garni. Process about half the beans in a food processor with 150ml/5 fl.oz water and stir into the sauce. Bring to the boil and let it simmer for 10 minutes before taking it from the heat and removing the bouquet garni. Stir in the remaining beans and season to taste. Cool.

TO FREEZE **Put the chops into a large casserole or one or two rigid freezer containers and pour over the sauce.**

TO DEFROST **Leave on the side for 12–14 hours or for 24–36 hours in the fridge.**

TO MICROWAVE **Follow your microwave instructions for defrosting and cooking the casserole.**

TO COOK **Before cooking make sure the meat is completely defrosted. Cook in the oven at 160°C/325°F/gas 3 for 1½–2 hours.**

TO SERVE **The casserole only needs one or two vegetables and definitely no potatoes as it is quite filling enough.**

❄ MOROCCAN LAMB COUSCOUS

The word couscous covers both the grain and the completed dish. It is traditionally cooked in a double-layered pot or steamer known as a *couscoussière*. The stew cooks in the large bulbous bottom half and when it is nearly ready the couscous is put to steam above it. Originally the couscous would have taken as long to cook as the stew but modern couscous, which as far as I know tastes as good, comes ready prepared, needing little more than soaking and heating.

Couscous is eaten all along the North African coast but is essentially Moroccan. The hot chilli paste, harissa, that adds guts and spice to my couscous usually comes in little tins or handy tubes.

This is a useful one-pot dish and needs no other accompaniments.

SERVES 6

1.3–1.5kg/3lb–3lb 5oz fresh boned shoulder of lamb

1 heaped teaspoon cinnamon

1 teaspoon ground ginger

½ teaspoon turmeric

1 teaspoon paprika

2 tablespoons olive oil

2 onions, peeled and chopped

425g/15oz can chickpeas, drained and rinsed

100g/3½oz dried apricots, halved

200g/7oz carrots, peeled and cut into chunks

200g/7oz fresh or frozen broad beans

1–2 teaspoons harissa

TO FINISH

50g/1¾oz flaked almonds

500g/1lb 2oz couscous

400ml/14fl oz boiling water

4 tablespoons olive oil

Cube the lamb. Combine the spices and oil in a bowl, add the lamb and stir it well in. Leave it to marinate for 1 hour then turn it into a sauté pan or deep frying pan and, stirring constantly over a medium heat, quickly brown it all over. Remove the meat, then add the onions, and, if necessary, a little more oil and cook until soft.

◆ Return the meat to the pan and add the chickpeas, apricots, carrots and broad beans. Pour in just enough water to cover the contents of the pan, bring to the boil and let it simmer for 5 minutes. Take the pan from the heat and stir in harissa paste to taste and season with salt. (If good wine is being served I don't like to produce a dish that is too hot and I find that a teaspoonful is about right, but you might find that rather insipid - you could use twice as much, according to your taste.) Leave to cool.

TO FREEZE **Leave in the casserole or turn into rigid freezer containers.**

TO DEFROST **Leave on the side for 8 hours or for 24 hours in the fridge.**

TO MICROWAVE **Follow your microwave instructions for defrosting and cooking the stew, then finish as below.**

TO COOK **If frozen in a freezer container, return to the casserole. Cook for 1½–2 hours with the oven set at 160°C/325°F/ gas 3. Check the casserole halfway through and add a little more water if the sauce seems to be evaporating.**

TO FINISH **Dry-toast the almonds to a nice nut brown, either in a frying pan or under the grill. Twenty minutes before you are due to eat, cook the couscous. Put it into a bowl and pour over hot water to cover. Leave it to soak for 10 minutes then separate the grains by forking them well. Transfer to a metal strainer and place over a pan of simmering water for 10 minutes. Mix the hot couscous with the olive oil and almonds and season.**

TO SERVE **Let everybody spoon a bed of couscous onto their plates and top it with the stew from the hot casserole.**

❄ LAMB STEAKS BAKED WITH KUMQUATS AND CORIANDER

This is a happy marriage of lamb with the sharp and fresh flavours of kumquats and coriander. This casserole also has the advantage of being easy on the cook, especially if it is prepared in an all-purpose dish which will take it to the freezer and, after defrosting, to the oven and then directly to table. As the meat is only partially cooked before freezing the defrosted casserole needs long slow cooking to ensure really tender and beautifully flavoured meat.

SERVES 6

4–5 tablespoons sunflower or groundnut oil

6 pieces fresh leg of lamb steak, about 100–125g/ 3^1/$_2$–4^1/$_2$oz each

3 onions, peeled and chopped

3 cloves garlic, peeled and chopped

5cm/2in piece ginger, peeled and chopped

200g/7oz kumquats

300ml/ ^{1}/$_2$ pint white wine

300ml/^{1}/$_2$ pint light chicken or vegetable stock

bunch coriander, chopped

40g/1^1/$_2$oz pinenuts

100g/3^1/$_2$oz fresh breadcrumbs

TO FINISH

handful coriander, chopped

Heat 2 tablespoons of the oil in a sauté pan and quickly brown the steaks on both sides. Remove the meat to a plate, sprinkle with a little salt and pepper and keep on one side.

◆ Lower the heat and, if necessary, pour in a little more oil to the pan. Add the onions, around two-thirds of the garlic and the ginger and cook, stirring occasionally, until soft. Purée the kumquats in a food processor, or chop them very finely, and stir them, together with the wine, the stock, half the coriander and seasoning to taste, into the softened onions. Cook for around 10-15 minutes to allow the flavours to amalgamate.

◆ Spread the sauce over the bottom of a shallow freezer- and ovenproof entrée or lasagne dish and place the meat on the top. In a dry frying pan quickly toast the pinenuts then stir them, the remaining garlic and coriander and some salt and pepper into the breadcrumbs. Spoon this mixture over the top of the meat and drizzle with a little oil.

TO FREEZE **Cover the dish tightly with foil or place it in a plastic bag.**

TO DEFROST **Leave on the side for 8–9 hours or for 20–24 hours in the fridge.**

TO MICROWAVE **Not suitable.**

TO COOK **Drizzle a little more oil over the top, cover with foil and bake at 160°C/ 325°F/gas 3 for 1^1/$_2$ hours, then increase the heat slightly, remove the foil, and cook for a further 15–20 minutes or until the top is bubbling and brown.**

TO FINISH **Sprinkle extra freshly chopped coriander over the top.**

❄ ITALIAN MEATBALLS IN MUSHROOM AND TOMATO SAUCE

Thinking that 'meatballs' might make you flip over the page muttering 'nursery food' under your breath, I contemplated giving this its Italian name, *Polpette di Agnello*. I finally decided that the dish is so good that it will stand up perfectly well to being served at any dinner party and to having an understandable English name.

I make the meatballs out of best quality leg of lamb steaks. You could use a cheaper cut, say shoulder with its wonderful sweet meat, but do cut off as much fat as you can.

SERVES 6

FOR THE SAUCE

250g/9oz button mushrooms, trimmed

200ml/7fl oz red wine

7 tablespoons olive oil

3 or 4 parsley stalks

juice ½ lemon

1 clove garlic, peeled and halved

1 large white onion, peeled and chopped

400g/14oz can chopped tomatoes

½ teaspoon ground coriander

1 teaspoon sugar

FOR THE MEATBALLS

600–750g/1lb5oz–1lb10oz leg of lamb steaks or trimmed boned shoulder

75g/2¾oz fresh breadcrumbs

1 egg

zest 1 lemon

25g/1oz parmesan, grated

bunch flat-leaf parsley

1 clove garlic

3 tablespoons olive oil

2 tablespoons flour

Start by making the sauce. Wipe (don't peel) the mushrooms with a damp cloth and slice them. In a large pan combine the wine with 4 tablespoons of the oil, the parsley stalks, lemon juice and garlic and pour in 200ml/7fl oz water.

◆ Bring to the boil and let it simmer for 5 minutes then add the mushrooms. Bring it back to boiling point, simmer for 10 minutes then use a slotted spoon to remove the mushrooms to a plate. Discard the parsley and garlic and reserve the liquid.

◆ Heat the remaining oil in a clean pan and sauté the onion until soft then add the tomatoes, the wine and oil mixture, the coriander and the sugar and season. Bring it back to the boil and let it simmer very gently for about 20 minutes or until the sauce has thickened and reduced. Take the pan from the heat and stir in the mushrooms.

◆ Leave the sauce on one side while you make the meatballs. Put the lamb, cut into chunks, in a food processor together with all the other ingredients, except for the oil and flour, and whizz up until the lamb is chopped and everything has amalgamated. In a frying pan heat a little of the oil and fry a small spoonful of the lamb. Taste and, if necessary, adjust the seasoning of the mixture. With wet hands take the mixture a spoonful at a time and roll into balls. The size you make is up to you, but I find that somewhere between the size of a walnut and a ping pong ball is about right. Lay them on a plate then sprinkle well with flour, turn them and sprinkle again. Heat more oil in the frying pan and fry the meatballs, fairly gently, until they are brown and cooked through. Remove to a plate covered in kitchen paper to soak up any extra oil.

◆ Put the cooked meatballs into the tomato sauce and stir to coat them with it. Leave until cold.

TO FREEZE **Turn into a shallow freezer- and ovenproof dish or into a rigid freezer container.**

TO DEFROST **Leave on the side for 5–7 hours or in the fridge overnight or up to 24 hours.**

TO MICROWAVE **Follow your microwave instructions for defrosting and reheating.**

TO REHEAT **Bake at 190°C/375°F/gas 5 for 30–40 minutes.**

❄ FILO-WRAPPED LAMB CUTLETS WITH MINT STUFFING

These little cutlets both look and taste a treat. They need to be trimmed of all fat and the bone scraped clean. You may be able to buy trimmed cutlets; otherwise buy a couple of prepared racks of best end and cut them carefully into individual cutlets yourself.

The mint-flavoured stuffing of crunchy hazelnuts and mushrooms is spooned onto the cutlets and then each one is wrapped in filo pastry and frozen. They are cooked after defrosting and you should finish up with a parcel of lovely crisp pastry, filled with succulent, perfectly cooked and slightly pink lamb.

SERVES 6

75g/2³/₄oz hazelnuts

140g/5oz mushrooms

100g/3¹/₂ oz butter

2 shallots, peeled and chopped

leaves from 2–3 sprigs fresh mint, chopped

sunflower oil for frying

12 fresh best end lamb cutlets, trimmed of all fat

12 sheets filo pastry

If necessary skin the hazelnuts by putting them on a tray in a hot oven for a few minutes and then rub off the skins in a tea towel.

◆ Dry-toast the hazelnuts either in a frying pan or put them back into the oven, on the tray, for 5 minutes. Put the browned nuts into a food processor and chop them, but not to a powder.

◆ Peel and destalk the mushrooms, chop finely and keep on one side.

◆ In a frying pan melt half the butter and cook the shallots until soft then transfer them to a bowl and mix in the mushrooms, nuts and mint, and season. Refrigerate until cold.

◆ Heat a little oil in the pan and quickly brown the cutlets on each side. You will probably have to do this in several batches, adding a little more oil each time.

◆ Melt the remaining butter, either in a pan or in the microwave and lay the filo pastry out on your work surface, covered with a damp tea towel. Keep it covered while you work with each sheet.

◆ Brush one sheet all over with butter then fold it in half lengthwise and brush again with butter. Put a cutlet, at an angle with the bone out sideways, about 5-7cm/2-2³/₄in from the bottom of the sheet and spoon some of the stuffing onto the cutlet. Bring the bottom piece of filo up over the cutlet and then roll it up. Seal the pastry on the meat side by brushing it with a little more butter and pressing any ends of pastry neatly together. Squash the pastry on the other side tightly round the bone, which will stick out like a handle. Repeat with the remaining cutlets.

TO FREEZE Put the cutlets in rigid freezer containers, separating them with grease-proof paper.

TO DEFROST Leave for 6–7 hours on the side or overnight in the fridge. Ensure the meat is completely defrosted before cooking the parcels.

TO MICROWAVE Not suitable.

TO COOK Preheat the oven to 200°C/400°F/gas 6 and cook the cutlets for up to 20 minutes, slightly less if you like your meat pink, but make sure the pastry is brown and crisp.

FILO-WRAPPED LAMB CUTLETS WITH MINT STUFFING

❄ CASSEROLE OF LAMB WITH LEMON, GARLIC AND ANCHOVIES

I think that a lamb casserole, such as this, with olive oil, lemon and garlic must have its origins in Greece but I am less sure about the authenticity of adding anchovies and capers. However the tasty combination is now well known, and justifiably so. I like to add to the Mediterranean mood by serving it with smoothly mashed potatoes flavoured with a little more garlic and a well-flavoured olive oil. I find it is easiest to buy good-sized ready-prepared lamb steaks but it would be more economical to buy a whole leg of lamb and to cut the meat off the bone.

SERVES 6

6 pieces fresh leg of lamb steak, about 100–125g/3¹⁄₂–4¹⁄₂oz each

1 Spanish onion, peeled and chopped

5 tablespoons olive oil

1 lemon, preferably unwaxed

50g1³⁄₄oz can anchovy fillets in oil, chopped

2 teaspoons capers, rinsed

300ml/10fl oz dry white wine

2 sprigs rosemary

TO COOK

2 cloves garlic, peeled and finely chopped

If using a joint, cut the meat from the bone and trim off any fat and skin. Cut the meat into cubes. If you are using ready-prepared steaks you could also cut them into cubes but I think they are nicer, as long as you have at least 6 good-sized ones, left whole.

◆ Sauté the onion in 3 tablespoons of the oil in a casserole or large saucepan until soft, then use a slotted spoon to remove it to a plate. Turn up the heat and quickly brown the meat. Lower the heat again, return the onion to the casserole, and add the zest and juice of the lemon, the chopped anchovies and their oil, the capers and wine and finally tuck in the rosemary sprigs.

◆ Bring the casserole to the boil, simmer gently for 20 minutes then season to taste. Use a slotted spoon to remove the meat and solids to a rigid freezer container (or, if you plan to freeze the lamb in the casserole, to a dish). Discard the rosemary sprigs and any stray needles that you can locate. Turn up the heat and bubble the sauce for 5 minutes or so until it has reduced and thickened a little. Either pour the sauce over the lamb in the freezer container or return the lamb to the casserole and leave until cold.

TO FREEZE **Cover with a lid or foil.**

TO DEFROST **Leave on the side for 7–8 hours or in the fridge for around 24 hours.**

TO MICROWAVE **Do not microwave if you have used a metal casserole, otherwise follow your oven's instructions for defrosting and cooking, adding the garlic as below.**

TO COOK **Stir the chopped garlic into the casserole then cook slowly in the oven at 160°C/325°F/gas 3 for 1¹⁄₂–2 hours. If the casserole was not completely defrosted cook for a little longer.**

❄ RAGOUT OF LAMB

Comfort food, yes, but very good comfort food. What could be better on a cold winter's evening?

SERVES 6

300g/10½oz baby onions or small shallots

200g/7oz lean unsmoked bacon, roughly chopped

2 tablespoons oil

800g/1lb 12oz fresh leg of lamb steaks, cubed

40g/1½oz flour

300ml/10fl oz red wine

400g/14oz can tomatoes

bouquet garni of parsley stalks, sprig thyme and bay leaf

350g/12oz button mushrooms, halved

Bring a small pan of water to the boil, add the onions, bring the water back to the boil and boil for 1 minute. Drain the onions, leave to cool a little then top and tail them and the skins will slip off easily.
◆ Heat a large metal casserole or a sauté pan, add the bacon and cook until all the fat has run. Remove the bacon from the pan, pour in the oil, turn up the heat, add the lamb and toss and stir it quickly to brown on all sides. Remove the lamb, turn down the heat slightly then add the onions and brown them all over. Return the bacon and lamb to the casserole, sprinkle on the flour, then pour in the wine and 100ml/3½fl oz water. Add the tomatoes, bouquet garni and mushrooms and season to taste. Bring to the boil and let it simmer for 10 minutes then remove from the heat and leave until cold.

TO FREEZE Freeze in the casserole or transfer to a rigid freezer container.
TO DEFROST Leave on the side for 7–8 hours or in the fridge for 16–18 hours.
TO MICROWAVE Follow your microwave instructions for defrosting and cooking then finish as below.
TO COOK Put the covered casserole in a low oven, 160°C/325°F/gas 3, for 1½–2 hours, or a little longer if the casserole was not completely defrosted.
TO FINISH Discard the bouquet garni.
TO SERVE Serve with mashed potatoes and a large green salad.

❄ PORK WITH PRUNES IN RED WINE SAUCE

Cooked slowly, this dish offers tender meat in a well-flavoured and balanced sauce.

SERVES 6

1 clove garlic, peeled

1 Spanish onion, peeled

50g/1¾oz butter

2 tablespoons olive oil

2 sprigs thyme

6 pork loin steaks

1 teaspoon sugar

1 tablespoon flour

1 tablespoon vinegar

75ml/2½fl oz red wine

250ml/9fl oz light stock

8–10 ready-to-eat prunes, stoned and halved

Roughly chop the garlic, halve and slice the onion.
◆ Put the butter, oil, garlic and thyme into a sauté or frying pan. Warm the pan and release the flavours of the garlic and thyme by pressing down hard on them with a wooden spoon then take them from the pan and discard. Raise the heat and quickly brown the pork on both sides. Remove the pork to a plate then stir in the onion and sugar. Fry until the onion has softened then sprinkle on the flour and one by one stir in the vinegar, wine and stock. Bring it all to the boil and stir until you have a smooth sauce. Season, add the prunes, then return the pork to the pan. Simmer for 3-4 minutes then take from the heat and leave to cool. (The sauce may seem quite thick, but you'll find that it will thin out during the final cooking.)

TO FREEZE Turn into a rigid freezer container or a freezer- and ovenproof gratin dish.
TO DEFROST Leave on the side for 6–7 hours or in the fridge for up to 24 hours.
TO MICROWAVE Follow your microwave instructions to defrost and cook the pork.
TO COOK Cook in a gratin dish, uncovered, at 150°C/300°F/gas 2 for 1¾–2 hours.

❄ HAM SAUPIQUET

Saupiquet des Amognes is a traditional French dish that is a speciality of the Nivernais and Morvan in central France and is said to have been created in the 16th century by one Jean Reynier, a culinary author. The piquant sauce or saupiquet – the name is derived from *sau*, salt and *piquet*, to season – has reduced wine and vinegar, juniper berries and tarragon among its ingredients and is used to coat thick slices of a mild ham. I think the dish is better if the sauce is not too assertive and I have used the mild and sweet raspberry vinegar which marries well with the ham.

The sauce can be frozen on its own, then, on the day of the party, defrosted and used to cover fresh slices of ham before it is all heated. Alternatively you can make up the whole dish ahead so that it simply needs defrosting and reheating on the day.

SERVES 6

50g/1³/₄oz butter

40g/1¹/₂oz plain flour

225ml/8fl oz mild ham or chicken stock

225ml/8fl oz dry white wine

6 juniper berries, lightly crushed

few sprigs tarragon, roughly chopped

5 shallots, peeled and chopped

150ml/5fl oz raspberry vinegar

10 peppercorns, lightly crushed

200ml/7fl oz double cream

600g/1lb 5oz unsmoked mild ham, thickly sliced

In a sauté pan melt the butter, stir in the flour, cook gently for a couple of minutes then stir in the stock and the wine. Bring to the boil, stirring until smooth. Add the juniper berries and tarragon and simmer, stirring occasionally, for 15 minutes.

◆ Meanwhile put the shallots, the vinegar and the peppercorns into a saucepan, bring to the boil and simmer until the vinegar has been reduced by three-quarters. Add to the sauce, stir to amalgamate and gently cook everything together for a further 15 minutes. Strain the sauce into a bowl, stir in the cream and adjust the seasoning, but remember that the ham might be quite salty and therefore you will need to add very little extra.

TO FREEZE **Turn the sauce into a rigid container and freeze it separately or lay the ham, trimmed of any excess fat, in a shallow dish and pour over the sauce before covering and freezing.**

TO DEFROST **Take either the sauce or the complete dish from the freezer and leave for at least 24 hours in the refrigerator.**

TO MICROWAVE **Defrost and reheat following the instructions for your oven.**

TO REHEAT **If you froze the sauce on its own use freshly sliced ham to make up the complete dish. Set the oven to 180°C/350°F/gas 4 and heat the dish, uncovered, for 25–30 minutes or until the sauce is hot and starting to bubble.**

TO SERVE **Serve with a salad or a green vegetable and a few little new potatoes.**

❄ PORK FILLET IN ORANGE AND PAPRIKA SAUCE

A friend of mine gave me her recipe for pork fillet in a paprika sauce and I then found a very similar one in Patricia Lousada's excellent book, *Easy to Entertain*. This is my interpretation of their two recipes. Pork tenderloin or fillet can be a meltingly tender piece of meat but it needs needs slow and careful cooking, or it will toughen up, so please adhere to the timings I have given. The meat is reheated in the sauce which, for a kitchen supper, you can leave as it is with the pieces of onion and pepper in it. For a more sophisticated dining-room dinner, and I prefer it, you can purée and sieve the sauce completely smooth.

I once made this in January and sharpened up the sauce with a Seville orange which was quite delicious but at other times use one of those smaller and sharper-flavoured oranges.

If you want to make this dish for 8 people increase the amount of meat to 1 kg/2lb 4oz but keep the sauce quantity exactly as given below.

SERVES 6

1 red pepper, halved, cored and deseeded

750–800g/1lb 10oz–1lb 12oz fresh pork fillet

3–5 tablespoons oil

1 Spanish onion, peeled and chopped

zest and juice 1 orange

1 tablespoon paprika

¼ teaspoon cayenne

50g/1³⁄₄oz plain flour

400ml/14fl oz light chicken or vegetable stock

2 teaspoons tomato purée

150ml/5fl oz thick plain yoghurt

Slice the pepper into very thin strips. Cut the pork, at an angle, into even slices.

◆ In a large sauté or frying pan heat 2 tablespoons of the oil and quickly, turning it once, brown the pork. You may need to do this in two batches, adding a little more oil for the second one. Remove the pork to a plate and keep on one side.

◆ Lower the heat, add a little more oil to the pan and sauté the pepper strips for about 5 minutes and when they are soft, stir in the onion and orange zest and sprinkle on the paprika and cayenne. Continue to cook, stirring occasionally for around 10 minutes, or until the onion is very soft, then stir in the flour followed by the stock, the orange juice and tomato purée. Season the sauce with salt, bring it to the boil and then let it simmer gently for a few minutes. Take the pan from the heat, and either leave the sauce as it is or whizz it all up in a food processor before passing it through a sieve. Stir in the yoghurt, adjust the seasoning and leave the sauce to cool.

◆ Spoon a little of the sauce into a shallow freezer- and ovenproof dish, arrange the slices of meat, neatly overlapping, and cover with the remaining sauce.

TO FREEZE **Cover the dish tightly with foil or a double layer of cling film.**

TO DEFROST **Leave for 7–8 hours on the side or for 15–18 hours in the fridge.**

TO MICROWAVE **Follow your microwave instructions for defrosting and cooking.**

TO COOK **Make sure the dish is at room temperature then cook at 150°C/300°F/ gas 2 for 1½–1³⁄₄ hours. You can then keep the dish warm in a very low oven.**

❄ PORK AND APPLE IN CALVADOS SAUCE

The ever-versatile pork fillet, here, Normandy-style, flamed with calvados which is then used in a sauce.

SERVES 6

750–800g/1lb10oz–1lb12oz fresh pork fillet

3 golden delicious apples, cored and peeled

75g/2³/₄oz butter

1 onion, peeled and thinly sliced

1 tablespoon oil

2 tablespoons calvados

1 tablespoon flour

300ml/10fl oz chicken stock

4 tablespoons double cream or crème fraîche

2 sage leaves

Cut each tenderloin into 6-8 slices. It is nice to have quite large slices of meat and the simplest way to do this is to cut them at an angle as if you were cutting thick slices of smoked salmon. Flatten the slices slightly by bashing them with a rolling pin then season with a little salt and pepper.

◆ Cut each cored apple into 4-5 round slices around the equator, as it were.

◆ In a large frying pan melt half the butter and sauté the onion until soft then remove from the pan with a slotted spoon. Add a little more butter and fry the apple slices, turning them once or twice, until golden and soft. Remove them to a plate, turn up the heat, add the remaining butter and the oil, and quickly brown the pork on both sides. Carefully pour the calvados over the pork and, standing well back, set light to it. Shake the pan until the flames have died down, take it from the heat and remove the meat to a plate. Return the onion to the pan, sprinkle on the flour and stir it in before pouring in the stock and bringing the sauce to the boil. Simmer for 2 minutes before adding the cream, the finely chopped sage leaves and seasoning to taste. Leave to cool.

TO FREEZE **Either put the pork into a shallow freezer- and ovenproof dish and pour over the sauce or transfer the pork and sauce to a rigid plastic container. Freeze the apples separately in a rigid container.**

TO DEFROST **Leave in the fridge for 20–24 hours.**

TO MICROWAVE **Not suitable.**

TO COOK **If you froze the meat in a plastic container remove it to an ovenproof dish. Put the apple slices into another dish and cover. Cook the pork at 150°C/300°F/ gas 2 for 1–1¹/₂ hours, putting the apple in to heat up for the last 20 minutes. You can keep it for a further ¹/₂ hour in a low oven.**

❄ BLANQUETTE DE PORC

This is my version of another traditional French casserole but it is one that nowadays only seems to appear on restaurant menus and seldom in the home. Perhaps the initial cooking of the meat sounds time-consuming and complicated and puts the cook off but, believe me, it isn't difficult, and the dish freezes well and tastes very good.

SERVES 6

750g/1lb 10oz pork shoulder steaks

700ml/1¼ pints light chicken stock or water

1 onion, peeled, studded with 3 cloves

1 carrot

bouquet garni of parsley stalks, strip of lemon rind and small bay leaf

175g/6oz baby onions

200g/7oz button mushrooms

85g/3oz butter

juice 1 lemon

40g/1½oz flour

TO FINISH

2 egg yolks

150ml/5fl oz crème fraîche or double cream

Cut the meat into pieces, put it into a pan and cover it with cold water. Bring up to the boil then drain and rinse the meat under a cold tap.

◆ Return the meat to the cleaned pan and add the stock or water and the onion, carrot and herbs. Bring to the boil and simmer gently, with the pan half-covered, for 40 minutes.

◆ Meanwhile put the baby onions into a pan of water, bring to the boil and simmer for 7-10 minutes or until tender. Drain, cool a little, then top and tail and slip the skins off.

◆ Trim off the base of the mushrooms and wipe them clean with a damp cloth. Melt half the butter in a frying pan and cook the mushrooms until golden brown on both sides then squeeze on the lemon juice and leave to cool.

◆ Drain the cooked meat, reserving the liquid, but discard the onion, carrot and herbs.

◆ Clean the pan and melt the remaining butter then stir in the flour and gradually add 700ml/1¼ pints of the cooking liquid. Stir until the sauce is smooth then let it gently simmer, with the occasional stir, for 15 minutes. Season to taste then take the pan from the heat and add the meat, the onions and the mushrooms and their juices.

TO FREEZE **Put in a freezer- and oven-proof casserole or rigid freezer container.**
TO DEFROST **Leave for 7–8 hours on the side or for up to 24 hours in the fridge.**
TO MICROWAVE **Follow your microwave instructions to defrost and reheat the meat then finish as below.**
TO REHEAT **Cook in the oven at 160°C/325°F/gas 3 for 1 hour.**
TO FINISH **Whisk the egg yolks into the crème fraîche or cream and gradually add to the hot casserole, stirring all the time. At this stage you can keep it hot for a while on the hob but over a low heat: don't let it boil or the sauce may separate.**

❄ CHEESE-AND-ANCHOVY-STUFFED INVOLTINI IN A WINE SAUCE

Involtini, stuffed bundles of pork, chicken or sometimes fish, are found all over Italy – varying according to the region. The cheese and anchovy stuffing is essentially from Puglia, right in the south of the country, where it is usually made with a local cheese called provola. You can substitute the more easily available tallegio or, failing that, bel paese.

Some supermarkets sell thinly sliced pork fillet which is ideal for this recipe but don't buy the wafer-thin slices that are sold for stir frying. Otherwise buy a pork fillet, slice it, put the slices between sheets of greaseproof paper, and then bash with a rolling pin to thin them out.

SERVES 6

1–2 slices fresh white bread

100g/3¹/₂oz tallegio or bel paese, roughly chopped

2 small sage leaves

50g/1³/₄oz anchovies in oil

85g/3oz butter

550g/1lb 4oz pork fillet, thinly cut into 12–18 slices

1 tablespoon flour

2 tablespoons oil

75ml/2¹/₂fl oz dry white wine

125ml/4fl oz light chicken stock

Put the bread, cheese and sage into a food processor and reduce to crumbs. Add the anchovies, some of their oil and a good grinding of pepper and process until they are chopped.

◆ Melt the butter in a large sauté pan, then turn off the heat. Lay a slice of the pork on your worktop and using a pastry brush, dip it into the melted butter and lightly brush over the slice of pork. Take a tablespoonful of the stuffing, squeeze it to make it hold together, place on the meat then roll it up and secure with a cocktail stick. Repeat with the remaining slices. Season the flour and sprinkle over the involtini.

◆ Add the oil to the butter in the pan, and return to the heat. Put in the involtini and sauté, turning them once or twice, until golden. Add the wine and let it bubble for 2-3 minutes before pouring in the stock and taking the pan from the heat. Leave until cold.

TO FREEZE **Put the involtini and sauce into a freezer- and ovenproof dish or a rigid freezer container.**

TO DEFROST **Leave for 5–6 hours on the side or for 14–15 hours in the fridge.**

TO MICROWAVE **Follow your microwave instructions to defrost and cook the involtini.**

TO COOK **If the involtini were frozen in a plastic container put them into an ovenproof dish. Make sure they are well covered with sauce. Cover the dish tightly and cook for 1¹/₄–1¹/₂ hours at 160°C/325°F/gas 3. If the involtini look as if they are drying up lower the temperature for the last ¹/₂ hour.**

CHEESE-AND-ANCHOVY-STUFFED INVOLTINI
IN A WINE SAUCE WITH GRATIN OF FENNEL AND
LEEKS (PAGE 125)

❄ FILLET OF BEEF EN CROUTE

This is a real treat and well worth cooking once in a while for that special lunch or dinner. You can season and flavour the meat in various ways: with horseradish as given below; with a few anchovies mashed up with some butter; or with 4-5 crushed garlic cloves blended into 100g (3¹/₂oz) butter with a handful of chopped parsley or mixed herbs, seasoned with salt and lots of pepper. Another tip from a friend, Jane Barne, is to sprinkle a few crushed pink peppercorns over the pastry and to roll them into it. (Jars of soft peppercorns in brine are found in many supermarkets.)

I tried cooking this from frozen but found that most of the meat got overcooked almost before the centre had defrosted so I would recommend that the parcel be thoroughly defrosted before it is cooked.

SERVES 6–8

2 tablespoons oil

1–1.2 kg/2lb 4oz–2lb 12oz fillet of beef

2 teaspoons hot grated horseradish

3 tablespoons double cream

500g/1lb 2oz packet puff pastry, defrosted

4–5 tablespoons semolina

Put the oven to heat to 200°C/400°F/gas 6.

◆ Heat the oil in a small roasting pan on the hob and quickly brown the meat all over. Put it into the oven and roast it for 10 minutes. Remove the meat from the oven and leave on the side until completely cold.

◆ Mix the horseradish into the cream and season well with salt and lots of freshly ground pepper.

◆ Roll the pastry out into a rectangle big enough to wrap easily around the meat. Sprinkle the semolina over the pastry (it is there to soak up the juices which in turn helps to keep the pastry crisp) and lightly roll it into the surface of the pastry. Dribble a little of the horseradish over the centre of the pastry, place the meat on top then spread the remaining horseradish over the meat. Cut a small square off each corner of the pastry then bring up the sides of the pastry and, using cold water, seal with a centre seam. Turn the end flaps up over the top and seal very carefully.

◆ If you wish, turn the parcel over and decorate the top with some trimmings from the pastry.

TO FREEZE **Wrap the pastry parcel very carefully with two layers of foil then place it in a plastic bag.**

TO DEFROST **Leave on the side for 12 hours or in the fridge for at least 24 hours.**

TO MICROWAVE **Not suitable.**

TO COOK **Set the oven to 220°C/425°F/ gas 7. Return the fully defrosted parcel, seam side down, to a roasting tray and cook for 35–45 minutes, depending on how red you like your beef. Take from the hot oven and leave to rest in a warm place for 10–15 minutes.**

TO SERVE **Cut into thick slices – 1 per person – and serve on hot plates, with a root vegetable purée such as parsnip and a fresh green vegetable. As it is wrapped in pastry I tend to dispense with potatoes.**

❄ DAUBE DE BOEUF PROVENCAL

The daube of Provence shows its more southerly origins by taking its name from the Spanish verb *dobar*, to braise. It is traditionally cooked in a beautifully shaped earthenware pot known as a *daubière* but it tastes much the same when cooked in a casserole.

The daube, I think, represents the best of French country cooking. The marination then slow cooking of the beef emphasises and melds the wonderful rich flavours incorporated in the dish.

SERVES 6–8

5 tablespoons olive oil

425ml/15fl oz rich red wine

2 cloves garlic, peeled, quartered and lightly crushed

1 bay leaf

4–5 sprigs thyme

2 cloves

thinly pared rind 1 orange

1.3kg/3lb chuck steak or other stewing beef, trimmed and cubed

225g/8oz thick cut streaky bacon, chopped

2 onions, peeled and chopped

2 tablespoons flour

600g/1lb 5oz ripe tomatoes, peeled, deseeded and roughly chopped

TO COOK

2 cloves garlic, peeled and chopped

rind ½ orange

3 sprigs thyme

In a large bowl mix 3 tablespoons of the oil with the wine, lightly crushed garlic, bay leaf, 3-4 sprigs thyme, cloves and three-quarters of the orange rind. Immerse the beef in this marinade and leave in the fridge for at least 12 and up to 24 hours.

◆ The following day, heat the remaining oil in a large sauté pan and cook the bacon and onion until the onion is soft. While it is cooking remove the meat from the marinade, picking off any clinging pieces of garlic or herb, and pat it dry with kitchen paper. Increase the heat then add the meat to the pan and stir and cook until it has browned on all sides, then sprinkle on the flour and cook for another 1-2 minutes. Transfer the meat to a large casserole then strain the marinade into the pan. Stir, scraping up any pieces on the bottom of the pan, until it comes to the boil and let it simmer 2 minutes. Pour this sauce over the meat then stir in the tomatoes, the remaining thyme and orange rind, and season.

◆ Put the casserole into a low oven, 160°C/325°F/gas 3, for 1½ hours. Check halfway through and if the liquid seems to have evaporated add a little water. Leave the casserole until cold.

TO FREEZE **Remove the orange rind and sprigs of thyme. Either freeze in the casserole or transfer the daube to a rigid freezer container.**

TO DEFROST **Leave on the side for 8 hours or in the fridge for at least 20 hours.**

TO MICROWAVE **Not suitable.**

TO COOK **Stir the garlic, the fresh orange rind and thyme into the daube and cook at 160°C/325°F/gas 3 for a further 2 hours.**

❄ PAUPIETTES OF BEEF ITALIAN-STYLE

The first recipe I ever had published was for paupiettes of beef and when thinking about this one I looked it up. It was a perfectly good traditional recipe with the paupiettes filled with sausage meat and flavourings, but for today's taste it sounds heavy and rather dull. For this new updated recipe I have gone Italian and filled the paupiettes with herbs, parmesan and grilled red peppers and cooked them in a tomato and wine sauce. I, for one, am very pleased with the update; the dish is much lighter, and the filling is both interesting and unexpected.

You can buy a piece of topside and slice it yourself or ask your butcher to do it for you. Use a piece of meat which has a large diameter.

SERVES 6

600–750g/1lb 5oz–1lb 10oz topside, cut into 6 even slices of about 100–125g/3½–4½oz each

1½ red peppers, quartered and deseeded

6 slices thin cut unsmoked streaky bacon

3 tablespoons parsley, finely chopped

2 tablespoons fresh oregano, finely chopped, or 1½ teaspoons dried oregano

1–2 cloves garlic, peeled and finely chopped

40g/1½oz parmesan, grated

2 tablespoons olive oil

1 onion, peeled and chopped

25g/1oz flour

400g/14oz can of chopped tomatoes

200ml/7fl oz white wine

TO REHEAT

2 garlic cloves, peeled and finely chopped

2 teaspoons fresh oregano, finely chopped, or 1 teaspoon dried oregano

1 tablespoon parsley, chopped

Put the beef slices between sheets of greaseproof paper and use a rolling pin to beat them out until they are nearly twice the size.

◆ Put the peppers, skin side up, on a sheet of foil under a hot grill. Grill, turning them round if necessary, until the skin is blackened and charred. Put the hot peppers into a plastic bag, seal the end, leave them to steam for around 20 minutes and then remove the skins.

◆ Stretch the bacon over the back of a knife and derind it if necessary. Blanch for 2 minutes in a pan of boiling water, drain, then cut each rasher into 2.

◆ Lightly season each slice of beef. Place 2 pieces of bacon on each slice then sprinkle with some parsley, oregano, garlic and parmesan. Put a quarter of red pepper on top then roll up carefully and secure with cocktail sticks.

◆ In a heavy casserole heat the oil, add the onion and cook gently for a few minutes to soften it. Turn up the heat, put in the paupiettes, quickly brown them on all sides and remove them from the casserole. At this point they might start to fall apart - you may need more cocktail sticks to do some running repairs. Reduce the heat, stir in the flour then add the tomatoes and the wine and season lightly. Then bring the sauce to the boil and let it simmer for 5 minutes. Leave until cold.

TO FREEZE **Return the beef to the casserole and freeze the complete dish or put it all into a rigid freezer container.**

TO DEFROST **Leave on the side for at least 8 hours or in the fridge for 24 hours.**

TO MICROWAVE **Not suitable.**

TO REHEAT **If frozen in a container return to the casserole. Add the garlic, oregano and parsley. Cover and cook for 2 hours at 160°C/325°F/gas 3. After the first hour turn over the paupiettes.**

TO FINISH **You will probably find that there is a lot of sauce, in which case take the paupiettes from the casserole and put them on a plate, covered, in a warm oven. Reduce the sauce and intensify its flavour by letting it bubble on the hob for 5 minutes or so, then check the seasoning. Remove the cocktail sticks from the paupiettes. They look attractive cut into slices for serving. Spoon the sauce onto the side.**

pasta & suppers

When I started writing this book, this chapter was intended to be called vegetarian dishes but as I worked on the other chapters I realised that quite a lot of those recipes are eminently suitable for vegetarians. I also wanted to include some family supper recipes, ones that were perhaps not quite appropriate for a party, but that make very good eating for any number of friends round the kitchen table and decided that this was the most suitable place for them. Hence the title for the chapter and the wide variety of recipes it contains. I have a vegetarian daughter for whom I frequently cook but I often divide the main mixture into two and add a little ham, bacon or whatever to one half. You will find that I have suggested both vegetarian and non-vegetarian options on those lines for several of the recipes.

❄ LASAGNE WITH ROASTED VEGETABLES ^v

Roasted vegetables make a delicious filling for lasagne and a very good vegetarian main course. I give the complete recipe, but the vegetables are exactly the same as used for the Roasted Mediterranean Vegetables on page 22, except that you need about half the quantity and need not add the olives and capers.

Lasagne sheets can become heavy and rather solid unless you first soak them in water. Also, frozen pasta absorbs more liquid than fresh, so I have given instructions for sauces that are quite thin.

SERVES 6–8

about 12 sheets lasagne

850ml/1½ pints milk

1 bay leaf

1 small aubergine

1 courgette

½ red onion

1 small red pepper

250g/9oz ripe plum tomatoes

5 tablespoons olive oil

3 canned or fresh baby artichoke hearts, quartered

2 cloves garlic, peeled and chopped

handful basil leaves

60g/2¼oz butter, plus extra for greasing the dish

60g/2¼oz flour

75g/2¾oz parmesan, freshly grated

1 mozzarella

Soak the lasagne sheets in a large bowl of warm water. Pour the milk into a pan, add the bay leaf and some salt and pepper, heat almost to boiling point and then remove from the hob and leave to infuse.

◆ Set the oven to heat to 220°C/375°F/gas 7 and prepare the vegetables. Dice the aubergine and courgette into bite-sized pieces and peel and roughly chop the onion. Deseed the pepper and cut the flesh into short strips. Skin the tomatoes and, depending on their size, leave them whole or cut into halves or quarters. Put all these vegetables into a roasting tin, sprinkle on some salt and pepper and drizzle over the oil. Put the tin into the hot oven and leave for 15 minutes then add the artichoke hearts, garlic and roughly torn basil leaves and give everything a good stir. Return the pan to the oven and leave for a further 15–20 minutes or until the vegetables are browning at the edge. Take the pan from the oven, pour in 150ml/5fl oz water, give everything another stir, adding, if necessary, a little more salt and pepper, then leave to cool.

◆ While the vegetables are in the oven, make the bechamel sauce. Melt the butter, stir in the flour and then strain in the cooled milk. Bring the sauce to the boil and whisk until smooth. The finished sauce needs to be quite thin; add a little more milk if necessary. Cook, stirring occasionally, for about 10 minutes then take from the heat, season and stir in about two-thirds of the parmesan.

◆ Drain the lasagne sheets and lay to dry on a clean tea towel. Thinly slice the mozzarella. Butter a deep rectangular freezer- and ovenproof lasagne dish well and smear a little of the bechamel over the bottom. Cover with a layer of the pasta and then spoon in half the vegetable mixture and spread slices of mozzarella over it. Cover with another layer of pasta, then half the remaining bechamel followed by more pasta, the rest of the vegetables and mozzarella, then a final layer of pasta and top it all with the rest of the bechamel and a generous sprinkling of parmesan.

TO FREEZE **Cover with foil.**

TO DEFROST **Leave for 8–10 hours on the side or for 24 hours in the fridge.**

TO MICROWAVE **Not suitable.**

TO COOK **Leave on the foil and cook at 180°C/350°F/gas 4 for 50–60 minutes, removing the foil halfway through to let the top brown lightly.**

❄ CANNELLONI STUFFED WITH SPINACH AND RICOTTA ᵛ

The combination of spinach and ricotta spiced up with a little nutmeg is frequently used in Italian dishes but it is one that never palls. The first time I experimented with this recipe was when my vegetarian daughter was coming to supper. In the end she got a better invitation so, thinking it would spoil, I put the cannelloni into the freezer. It was a winner: the stuffing remained moist and the cream sauce retained not only its consistency but its lovely fresh taste.

I much prefer to use fresh spinach; however good the frozen leaves are, the fresh ones have the edge. If you do use frozen, let it defrost then squeeze out the moisture before whizzing it up with the cheeses.

I also recommend pre-cooking the cannelloni. I know the tubes are easier to stuff direct from the packet but you will then need to add at least twice as much sauce as they will really soak it up when cooking. Uncooked ones are, especially if they are to be frozen, still inclined to remain rather dry and heavy.

You may also think that the sauce, being virtually undiluted cream, sounds rather rich. However, it is only single cream and it is going to be divided amongst several people and, to compensate, ricotta is very low in fat. I have used cream, rather than the more usual bechamel, as it makes a much lighter, fresher-tasting, more party-like dish.

SERVES 3 AS A MAIN COURSE,
6 AS A STARTER,

400g/14oz fresh spinach

250g/9oz ricotta

35g/1¼oz parmesan, grated

½ teaspoon nutmeg, ground

12 cannelloni tubes

50g/1¾oz butter

300ml/10 fl oz single cream

Wash the spinach well and discard any tough stalks. Pack it all into a saucepan and cook, turning occasionally, until it has boiled down and softened. You can also cook spinach successfully in a microwave: either put it back into the supermarket pack it came in, turn under the ends and put on a plate, or pack it into a large bowl and cover with cling film. Prick the pack or cling film a few times and microwave on high for 3½ minutes. Turn the spinach into a colander, leave to cool and then squeeze out as much water as you can.

◆ Put the spinach, ricotta and parmesan with a pinch of nutmeg and salt and pepper into a food processor or blender and whizz together.

◆ Cook the cannelloni in a large pan of boiling salted water for around 8 minutes, or until al dente. Drain and rinse well under a running cold tap. Fill the cannelloni with the spinach mixture: the easiest way to do this is with a piping bag using a large plain nozzle, but alternatively you can push the filling in using a small teaspoon. Put a single layer of cannelloni in a shallow freezer- and ovenproof dish. It doesn't matter if they are squashed up tightly.

◆ In a small pan heat the butter and cream and let it simmer for 2-3 minutes.

◆ Spoon the cream over the cannelloni, covering each one, but let any excess sauce run down into the dish. Leave until cold.

TO FREEZE **Cover the dish tightly with a piece of foil.**

TO DEFROST **Leave on the side for 7–8 hours or overnight or longer in the fridge.**

TO MICROWAVE **Follow the instructions for your microwave to defrost and/or reheat.**

TO REHEAT **Heat in an oven preheated to 190°C/375°F/gas 5 for 30 minutes.**

❄ PASTA WITH SAUSAGE AND TOMATO SAUCE

Use a country-style pork sausage such as the French Toulouse sausage found in supermarkets.

SERVES 4–6

5 tablespoons olive oil

1 large onion, peeled and finely sliced

2 x 400g/14oz cans chopped tomatoes

1 teaspoon sugar

2 cloves garlic, peeled and sliced

6–8 basil leaves, chopped

450g/1lb sausages

TO FINISH

500g/1lb 2oz fusilli or conchiglie

Heat 2 tablespoons of the oil in a pan and gently fry the onion, stirring occasionally, until it is yellow. Add the tomatoes, sugar, garlic, basil, 2 more tablespoons of olive oil and seasoning. Bring it to the boil and simmer for around $^1/_2$ hour or until the flavours have mellowed and the sauce has reduced and thickened.

◆ Meanwhile skin the sausages. The easiest way to do this is to hold each one under a cold tap and use a sharp knife to slit the skin from top to bottom. It will then just peel off.

◆ Cut the sausages into bite-sized pieces. Heat the remaining tablespoon of oil in a non-stick pan and fry the sausage until brown.

◆ Remove the cooked tomato sauce from the heat and stir in the sausages, including any scrapings from the pan. Leave until cold.

TO FREEZE **Turn the sauce into a rigid freezer container.**

TO DEFROST **Leave on the side for 6–7 hours or in the fridge for 15 hours.**

TO MICROWAVE **Follow the instructions for your microwave to defrost and reheat.**

TO REHEAT **Reheat the sauce gently.**

TO FINISH **Cook the pasta, drain it, reserving a cup of cooking liquid. Turn it into a serving dish. Pour over the sauce and mix, adding cooking liquid if necessary.**

TO SERVE **Offer grated parmesan.**

❄ PASTA WITH PEPPER AND ANCHOVY SAUCE

SERVES 6

4 large peppers, red, yellow, orange or mixed

2 tablespoons olive oil

2 cloves garlic, peeled and sliced

50g/1³/₄oz can anchovy fillets

400g/14oz can chopped tomatoes

75g/2³/₄oz black olives, halved and stoned

TO FINISH

600g/1lb 5oz spaghetti or spaghettini

50g/1³/₄oz dry white breadcrumbs

2 tablespoons flat-leaf parsley, chopped

2 tablespoons olive oil

Halve the peppers, remove the seeds and core. Grill them, skin side up, until they are cracked and blackened then immediately put them into a plastic bag, seal it and leave for 20 minutes. Take the cooled peppers from the bag, peel off the skin and chop the flesh into narrow strips.

◆ In a sauté pan heat the oil, add the garlic and the anchovies and cook very gently, squashing the anchovies down with a wooden spoon to reduce them to a paste. Pour in the tomatoes and simmer for 15 minutes to reduce the sauce slightly. Add the pepper strips and simmer everything together for 10 minutes. Take the pan from the heat, stir in the olives and check the seasoning. Leave until cold.

TO FREEZE **Turn the sauce into a rigid freezer container.**

TO DEFROST **Leave for 5–6 hours on the side or for 15–18 hours in the fridge.**

TO MICROWAVE **Follow the instructions for your microwave to defrost and reheat.**

TO REHEAT **Reheat the sauce gently.**

TO FINISH **Cook the pasta, drain it, reserving a cupful of the cooking liquid. Turn the pasta into a serving dish, pour over the sauce and mix together. If it seems dry add some of the reserved cooking liquid. Scatter the breadcrumbs and the parsley over the pasta, drizzle on the oil and toss.**

PASTA WITH PEPPER AND ANCHOVY SAUCE

❋ PASTA WITH MUSHROOM SAUCE ⱽ

An intensely flavoured sauce and one that distributes itself beautifully in the folds of tagliatelle.

SERVES 4

25g/1oz dried porcini mushrooms

400g/14oz fresh mushrooms: brown, field and oyster

2 cloves garlic, peeled

2 tablespoons olive oil

25g/1oz butter

3 tablespoons parsley, chopped

3 tablespoons sherry

1 tablespoon cornflour

3 tablespoons milk

TO FINISH

450g/1lb tagliatelle

Soak the porcini in 300ml/10fl oz water for ½ hour, strain and keep the liquid. Trim the mushrooms, wipe with a damp cloth and slice.
◆ Chop the garlic. Heat 1 tablespoon of the oil in a pan and gently sauté the porcini for 4-5 minutes. Add the remaining oil and the butter and when it has melted stir in the garlic and parsley. Cook for 1 minute then turn up the heat and add the mushrooms. Keep stirring until the mushrooms start to ooze moisture then add the sherry and the reserved liquid. Bring to the boil and simmer for 7-8 minutes.
◆ Slake the cornflour in the milk and add it a spoonful at a time to the simmering mixture. You may not need it all, so stop when the sauce has a good consistency and colour with a sheen to it. Season to taste. Leave until cold.

TO FREEZE **Turn the sauce into a rigid freezing container.**

TO DEFROST **Leave on the side for 4–5 hours or overnight in the fridge.**

TO MICROWAVE **Follow the instructions for your microwave to defrost and reheat.**

TO REHEAT **Heat the sauce slowly in a pan, and simmer for a few minutes.**

TO FINISH **Cook and drain the pasta, reserving a cup of cooking liquid. Transfer to a serving dish and pour over the sauce. Stir and, if necessary, add some reserved cooking liquid. Serve immediately.**

❋ MUSHROOM AND POLENTA 'LASAGNE' ⱽ

This unusual dish is layered in the same way as traditional lasagne, using polenta instead of lasagne.

SERVES 6

300g/10½oz polenta flour

25g/1oz butter

25g/1oz flour

450ml/16fl oz milk

75g/2¾oz parmesan, grated

1 quantity Mushroom Sauce (above)

In a pan boil 1.2 litres/2 pints of water and add 1 teaspoon salt. Remove from the heat and slowly add the polenta, stirring all the time to prevent lumps forming. Cook on the hob, stirring, for 5 minutes. Transfer the polenta to a greased baking dish. Smooth over and leave until cold.
◆ To make a bechamel, melt the butter, stir in the flour and slowly add the milk. Boil and, stirring, cook for 3-4 minutes. Remove from heat and stir in 50g/2oz of the grated parmesan. Season to taste.
◆ Cut the polenta into squares. Grease a deep freezer- and ovenproof dish and pour in half the bechamel. Cover with a layer of polenta squares then pour over the mushroom sauce and cover with a further layer of polenta. Pour on the remaining bechamel and sprinkle with the remaining parmesan.

TO FREEZE **Cover with foil or a double layer of cling film.**

TO DEFROST **Leave on the side for 7–8 hours or in the fridge for at least 18 hours.**

TO MICROWAVE **Not suitable.**

TO REHEAT **Preheat the oven to 180°C/350°F/gas 4 and bake the polenta uncovered for 40–45 minutes or until the top is browned and bubbling.**

❄ PASTA CASSEROLE WITH AUBERGINES AND TOMATOES ᵛ

This pasta dish has long been a family favourite and is perfect, served with a large green salad, for an informal evening round the kitchen table.

SERVES 3–4 AS A MAIN COURSE, 6 AS A STARTER,

2 medium or 1 large aubergine

2 Spanish or sweet onions, peeled and chopped

6–8 tablespoons olive oil

3–4 cloves garlic, peeled and chopped

2 x 400g/14oz cans chopped tomatoes

1 red pepper, deseeded and cored

300g/10^1/₂oz pasta shapes, farfalle or similar

25g/1oz parmesan, grated

4 slices stale bread

Top and tail the aubergines and cut into cubes. Put them into a sieve, sprinkle with salt and leave to drain.

◆ In a large pan sauté the onions in 2 tablespoons of the oil until soft. Stir in half the chopped garlic then the tomatoes. Cook for 10-15 minutes then remove the pan from the heat.

◆ Meanwhile cut the pepper into short strips. In another frying pan heat 1 tablespoon of oil and cook the pepper until it is softening. Rinse the aubergine cubes under a cold tap, drain, and dry them in a clean tea towel. Add the cubes to the pepper and fry over a fairly high heat until they are soft and golden. You will need to stir frequently and you may need to add a further splash or two of oil.

◆ Bring a large pan of salted water to the boil and, following the packet instructions, cook the pasta until al dente. Drain the cooked pasta in a sieve and, to stop it sticking together, rinse it well under a running cold tap. Return the pasta to the rinsed-out pan then add the aubergine mixture, the tomato sauce and parmesan, mix together and season to taste.

◆ Put the bread into a food processor and reduce it to crumbs. In a frying pan heat 3 tablespoons of oil and fry the breadcrumbs. As they start to change colour stir in the rest of the garlic and a little salt. Continue cooking the mixture until the crumbs turn golden then remove the pan from the heat.

TO FREEZE **Transfer the pasta mixture to a freezer- and ovenproof casserole and spoon the breadcrumb mixture over the top. Cover tightly with foil or a double layer of cling film.**

TO DEFROST **Leave on the side for 9–10 hours or in the fridge for at least 18 hours.**

TO MICROWAVE **Not suitable.**

TO REHEAT **Heat the oven to 180°/350°/gas 4 and cook the casserole for 40–45 minutes or until it is bubbling.**

TO SERVE **Hand round a good-sized bowl of parmesan and a large green salad.**

❄ GNOCCHI ALLA ROMANA CON SALVIA ⱽ

I remember once being in Rome with my parents and eating the most sublime plates of gnocchi for lunch in a trattoria. My parents returned to Rome a year or so later and went back to the trattoria where they were greeted like old friends but told that they had come on the wrong day of the week: self-respecting Romans only ate gnocchi on Thursdays.

There are many different types of gnocchi and this, the Roman one, is made with semolina, which I think is one of the best. It is also delicious turned into croquettes (see opposite) and served as a first course or alongside a main course.

I like the simple and traditional way of serving gnocchi with parmesan and sage but I do often turn it into a non-vegetarian dish by adding some fried and chopped pancetta or some ham. You can also ring the changes by using basil instead of sage and making a tomato sauce.

SERVES 4 AS A MAIN COURSE,
6–8 AS A STARTER

FOR THE GNOCCHI

1 litre/1³⁄₄ pints milk

200g/7oz semolina

50g/1³⁄₄oz butter

50g/1³⁄₄oz parmesan, grated

75g/2³⁄₄oz chopped pancetta, fried, or chopped ham (optional)

3 egg yolks

2–3 leaves sage, finely chopped

1 teaspoon Dijon mustard

FOR THE TOPPING

50g/1³⁄₄oz butter

2 cloves garlic, peeled and lightly crushed

6 sage leaves

50g/1³⁄₄oz parmesan, grated

To make the gnocchi bring the milk to boiling point, then, in a steady stream to avoid lumps, add the semolina. Stir hard with a wooden spoon - it will bubble like Vesuvius - until it is smooth. Take from the heat and leave to cool a little. Stir in the butter, parmesan and, if using, the pancetta or ham. Leave it to cool then add the egg yolks, chopped sage and mustard and season well.

◆ Turn it into a well-greased shallow dish or swiss roll tin and spread it flat with a palette knife dipped in water. Leave until completely cold.

◆ To prepare the topping melt the butter and add the lightly crushed garlic cloves and the sage and leave to infuse.

◆ Cut the gnocchi into rounds using a pastry cutter or, even easier, score the tin into diamonds. Arrange these shapes, overlapping, in a well-greased gratin or shallow freezer- and ovenproof dish and fill any holes or corners with any odd pieces that may be left.

◆ Strain over the butter and sprinkle the cheese on the top.

TO FREEZE **Cover with foil or a double layer of cling film.**

TO DEFROST **Leave on the side for 7–8 hours or in the fridge for 16–18 hours.**

TO MICROWAVE **Not suitable.**

TO REHEAT **Bake uncovered in a pre-heated oven at 200°C/400°F/gas 6 for 30–35 minutes or until everything is hot and a golden crust has formed. Leave to cool for a few minutes before serving.**

❄ CROQUETTES DE GNOCCHI ROMANA ⱽ

These gnocchi croquettes make a lovely and unusual accompaniment to a main course. They can also be served by themselves as a first course when I would accompany them with some hot tomato sauce.

SERVES 6–8

1 quantity of the mixture for Gnocchi alla Romana con Salvia (opposite)

1 tablespoon flour, seasoned with salt and pepper

1 beaten egg

50g/1³/₄oz breadcrumbs

sunflower oil for frying

Follow the recipe opposite for the gnocchi and when the mixture is spread out in a tin leave until completely cold.

◆ Use a spoon to scoop out the mixture and then with wet hands shape into croquettes about 5cm/2in long and the diameter of a fat carrot. Sprinkle the flour onto a board, roll the croquettes in it, then brush all over with egg and finally roll them in the breadcrumbs.

◆ Fry them either in a deep fat fryer or in a frying pan with 1cm/¹/₂in oil in it, turning them over to brown on all sides. Drain the hot croquettes on kitchen paper and leave until cold.

TO FREEZE **Pack in rigid freezer containers.**

TO DEFROST **Take as many as you need from the freezer and leave on the side for 2–3 hours or in the fridge for 5–6 hours.**

TO REHEAT **Lay the croquettes on a baking sheet and heat at 200°C/400°F/gas 6 for 20 minutes or until very hot.**

❄ TOMATO AND PASTA GRATIN ⱽ

This makes a good light vegetarian main course or it could also be served as a first course. Like all dishes made with fresh tomatoes it should really be made in the summer or early autumn when they are at their best.

SERVES 4 AS A MAIN COURSE, 6 AS A STARTER

300g/10¹/₂oz pasta shapes, farfalle or similar

125g/4¹/₂oz gruyère

1 tablespoon olive oil

20g/³/₄oz butter

1 Spanish onion, peeled and sliced

2 cloves garlic, peeled and chopped

2 tablespoons flour

750g/1lb 10oz tomatoes, peeled and roughly chopped

60g/2¹/₄oz parmesan, grated

bunch basil, chopped

3 eggs

6 tablespoons fresh breadcrumbs

Cook the pasta until it is al dente in a pan of boiling salted water. Drain the pasta then immediately rinse it under a cold tap. Keep on one side until needed. Cube the gruyère.

◆ Heat the oil and butter in a frying or sauté pan and cook the onion and garlic for 2–3 minutes, stir in the flour then the tomatoes. Cook for 2 minutes before taking the pan from the heat and stirring in the pasta, the gruyère, about three-quarters of the parmesan, and the basil. Break in the eggs, mix them in and season to taste.

◆ Spoon everything into a shallow freezer- and ovenproof dish. Mix the breadcrumbs with the remaining parmesan and lightly season. Sprinkle them over the top.

TO FREEZE **Cover the dish with foil or a double layer of cling film.**

TO DEFROST **Leave on the side for 5–7 hours or in the fridge for 15 hours.**

TO MICROWAVE **Defrost and heat following the instructions for your oven.**

TO REHEAT **Put in an oven preheated to 190°C/375°F/gas 5 for 25–30 minutes or until the top is bubbling and brown.**

❄ PEPPERS STUFFED WITH COUSCOUS ⱽ

For this dish I have mixed the cuisines from both sides of the Straits of Gibraltar. In southern Spain peppers are often cooked with olive oil and, across the sea, couscous is the staple food of Morocco. This dish makes a good vegetarian main course but does equally as a first course.

I was in Tangier recently, and bought the most wonderful bulbous earthenware *couscoussière*. The pot is very decorative and I am not sure that I will ever sum up the courage to soak it in water, oil it and then cook in it. Never mind, for this recipe, the couscous just needs soaking in water and the peppers baking in the oven.

Small tins or convenient tubes of the North African hot chilli paste, harissa, can be found in specialist shops and some supermarkets. You could replace it with chilli flakes or powder and a little more garlic.

SERVES 4 AS A MAIN COURSE, 6 AS A STARTER

3–4 large peppers or 6 small ones, various colours

about 2 teaspoons harissa, according to taste

250g/9oz couscous

4 tablespoons raisins

40g/1¹⁄₂oz flaked almonds

1 clove garlic, peeled

4–6 tablespoons olive oil

¹⁄₂ teaspoon ground cinnamon

2 tablespoons flat-leaf parsley, chopped

TO REHEAT

a little olive oil

Heat the oven to 180°C/350°F/gas 4 and bake the peppers, whole, for 30 minutes. Take them from the oven and leave until cool.

◆ Pour 300ml/10fl oz very hot water into a bowl and stir in the harissa. Add the couscous and leave to soak for 15 minutes. Cover the raisins with hot water and leave them to soak. Toast the almonds either under the grill or in a frying pan. Squash the garlic and sauté it very gently in 4 tablespoons of olive oil.

◆ Fluff up the couscous with a fork then pour on the oil, straining out the garlic, and use your hands to rub the couscous to make sure that all the grains are separate. Mix in the drained raisins, the almonds, cinnamon and parsley and season well. If the couscous seems to be on the dry side stir in more olive oil.

◆ Halve the cooled peppers and remove all the seeds and membrane but leave the stalk intact as it helps to keep the shape. Pack them into a shallow freezer- and ovenproof dish and fill each one with couscous.

TO FREEZE **Cover with foil or a double layer of clingfilm.**

TO DEFROST **Leave on the side for 6–7 hours or in the fridge for 15–16 hours.**

TO MICROWAVE **Follow your microwave instructions to defrost and reheat.**

TO REHEAT **Drizzle olive oil over the peppers then cover with foil. Heat in the oven at 190°C/375°F/gas 5 for 20–25 minutes.**

❄ MOUSSAKA

A well-tried supper dish that freezes like a dream. In the Middle East moussaka is always pepped up with cinnamon and allspice; I include them in the recipe but omit them if you prefer it plain.

SERVES 6

3 medium aubergines

1 large onion, peeled and thinly sliced

4 tablespoons sunflower oil

650g/1lb 7oz minced lamb

2 tomatoes, peeled and chopped

125ml/4fl oz dry white wine

1 teaspoon ground cinnamon

pinch allspice

2 tablespoons parsley, chopped

70g/2¹/₂oz butter

70g/2¹/₂oz flour

600ml/1 pint milk

50g/1³/₄oz parmesan, grated

pinch nutmeg, grated

2 eggs

Top and tail the aubergines, cut them into slices lengthwise, sprinkle lightly on both sides with salt and leave them to drain.

◆ Meanwhile make the meat sauce. Fry the onion in 2 tablespoons of oil and when it is soft and golden add the meat and stir until well browned. Add the tomatoes, wine, cinnamon, allspice, parsley and seasonings and simmer for 15-20 minutes, stirring frequently. You want to finish with the meat very dry so only add water if it starts to stick or burn.

◆ Gently squeeze some of the bitter juices from the aubergines, put them in a colander and rinse under a cold tap. Dry them with a clean tea towel or kitchen paper. Heat the remaining oil, adding more if necessary, and fry the aubergine slices until light brown on both sides and drain on a double layer of kitchen paper.

◆ In a clean pan melt the butter, stir in the flour and when it has amalgamated slowly add the milk. Stirring, bring to the boil and simmer for 4-5 minutes then add half the parmesan and season with salt, pepper and a little grated nutmeg and take the pan from the heat. In a small bowl whisk the eggs together with a little of the bechamel sauce. Stirring constantly, pour the egg mixture back into the pan and stir until thickened.

◆ Cover the base of a roasting tin or large freezer- and ovenproof lasagne dish with a layer of aubergine slices and sprinkle with half the remaining parmesan. Spread half the meat mixture on the top, then another layer of aubergines, the remaining parmesan and the meat. Top with aubergine slices then pour the bechamel sauce over the top. Leave until cold.

TO FREEZE **Cover with a double layer of cling film or foil.**

TO DEFROST **Leave on the side for 7–8 hours or in the fridge for 18–20 hours.**

TO MICROWAVE **Follow the instructions for your microwave to defrost and reheat.**

TO REHEAT **The moussaka can be cooked from frozen or half frozen but increase the cooking times if you do this. Bake at 180°C/350°F/gas 4 for 45–50 minutes or until the top is bubbling and browned.**

❄ FILO VEGETABLE PIE ⱽ

I have added my favourite saffron to the sauce for this mixed vegetable pie but, in a less extravagant mood, you could replace it with a good handful of chopped parsley. The resulting pie would be very different but still good.

I have chosen the vegetables because none of them has a very strong or dominant flavour, so they are well matched. You could change the mixture but keep in mind that the vegetables need to complement each other, and try to choose ones that won't disintegrate in the sauce.

To ensure the filo pastry cooks on the bottom properly I use a metal quiche tin. You need a fairly deep one, with a diameter about 25-30cm/10-12in.

SERVES 4 AS A MAIN COURSE, 6 AS A STARTER

150g/5½oz baby onions

100g//3½oz baby carrots

100g/3½oz mangetouts

100g/3½oz baby sweetcorn

100g/3½oz fresh asparagus or packet asparagus tips

2 pinches saffron

75g/2¾oz butter

50g/1¾oz flour

450ml/16fl oz milk

150ml/5fl oz white wine

150ml/5fl oz double cream

200g/7oz frozen peas

8–12 sheets, depending on size, filo pastry, defrosted if frozen

Plunge the baby onions into a pan of boiling water and simmer for 8 minutes. Drain and when they are cool remove the roots and skins.

◆ Top and tail the carrots and cook for 6-8 minutes or until tender. Top and tail the mangetouts and cook them together with the sweetcorn for 3 minutes, then add the asparagus and cook for a further 4 minutes or until just tender.

◆ Cut the carrots, sweetcorn and asparagus into bite-sized pieces. Leave the saffron to infuse in a bowl of 100ml/3½fl oz hot water.

◆ Melt 50g/1¾oz of the butter, stir in the flour then slowly add the milk then the wine. Cook until you have a smooth thick sauce then add in the saffron and its liquid and the cream. Take the pan from the heat, season to taste and stir in all the prepared vegetables and the frozen peas. Keep until needed.

◆ Melt the butter, lay out the filo sheets and cover with a damp cloth. Brush the inside of the quiche tin with butter. Take a sheet of the pastry, brush it all over with butter, fold it in half, butter side in, and brush both outer sides with butter. Lay it in the tin with the ends hanging over the sides. Repeat, putting the sheets in at an angle, with another 3-6 sheets of the pastry. You need to finish with a solid base and enough overhanging pastry to fold back on the filling.

◆ Spoon in the filling then fold the overhanging pieces of pastry back over it. Butter another sheet of pastry and, crumpling it into folds, cover part of the top of the pie. Repeat with further pastry until the pie is completely covered.

▼ This dish isn't difficult to make and it can be done in stages. If you are short of time you can cook the vegetables 24 hours ahead and keep them in a covered dish in the fridge.

TO FREEZE **Slip the pie into a plastic bag and put it in the freezer. Remember not to put anything else on top of it.**
TO DEFROST **It is best cooked when it is partially defrosted and I leave it in the fridge for 5–8 hours.**
TO MICROWAVE **Not suitable.**
TO COOK **Cover the pie loosely with foil and cook in a preheated oven, 200°C/400°F/gas 6, for ¾–1½ hours, depending on how frozen the pie was when put into the oven. Test with a skewer to make sure the centre is fully defrosted then remove the foil for the last 10 minutes to get the pastry crisp and brown.**

❄ STUFFED TOMATOES WITH PINENUTS AND PARMESAN ᵛ

Stuffed tomatoes freeze surprisingly well, as these two recipes demonstrate.

SERVES 4 AS LIGHT MAIN
COURSE, 4–8 AS A STARTER

8 good-sized ripe tomatoes

2 shallots, peeled and finely chopped

1–2 cloves garlic, peeled and chopped

3 tablespoons olive oil

150g/5¹/₂oz fresh breadcrumbs

2 tablespoons pinenuts

2 tablespoons parmesan, grated

small bunch parsley, chopped

1 teaspoon oregano, chopped, or ¹/₂ teaspoon dried oregano

Wipe the tomatoes clean then cut a lid off each one and reserve. Spoon out and keep all the flesh and pulp from the cavity, sprinkle a little salt inside each shell and leave upside down to drain for about ¹/₂ hour.

◆ Remove as many seeds as you can and roughly chop the remaining flesh.

◆ Fry the shallots and garlic in the olive oil until soft then add the breadcrumbs and pinenuts and, stirring frequently, continue frying until the breadcrumbs are golden and crisp. Remove the pan from the heat and stir in the tomato flesh, parmesan, parsley and oregano and season to taste.

◆ Wipe the salt out of the shells with kitchen paper then spoon the mixture into them. Put back the lids.

TO FREEZE **Pack the tomatoes into a rigid freezer container.**

TO DEFROST **Leave on the side for 2–3 hours or in the fridge for 6–8 hours.**

TO MICROWAVE **Not suitable.**

TO COOK **Put the tomatoes into a small roasting pan, brush them over with oil and cook in the oven at 180°C/350°F/gas 4 for 30 minutes, or slightly longer if they were not completely defrosted.**

❄ STUFFED TOMATOES WITH PANCETTA AND MUSHROOMS

SERVES 4–8 AS A STARTER,
4 AS LIGHT MAIN COURSE

8 good-sized ripe tomatoes

2 tablespoons olive oil

125g/4¹/₂oz pancetta or smoked streaky bacon rashers, chopped

1 shallot, peeled and chopped

1 clove garlic, peeled and chopped

150g/5¹/₂oz fresh breadcrumbs

50g/1³/₄oz button mushrooms, finely chopped

1 tablespoon parsley, chopped

Prepare the tomatoes as in the above recipe.

◆ In a frying pan heat the oil and gently fry the pancetta or bacon until the fat has been released, then add the shallot and garlic and continue frying until soft. Stir in the breadcrumbs and cook until golden, then add the mushrooms and cook for a further 2 minutes to soften them. Remove the pan from the heat and stir in the reserved tomato flesh and the parsley and season to taste.

◆ Wipe the shells out with a piece of kitchen paper then spoon the mixture into them and put back the lids.

TO FREEZE **Pack the tomatoes into a rigid freezer container.**

TO DEFROST **Leave on the side for 2–3 hours or in the fridge for 6–8 hours.**

TO MICROWAVE **Not suitable.**

TO COOK **Put the tomatoes in a roasting pan, brush with oil and cook in the oven at 180°C/350°F/gas 4 for 30 minutes, or longer if they were not completely defrosted.**

SPINACH AND SPICY POTATO TART ᵛ

Spinach always makes a good base to a quiche or tart and for this one I have added some diced potatoes and onion spiced up with a little garam masala and chilli. You only need to use a little garam masala and a little or no chilli as I think the tart is nicest if the spicy taste is pleasantly subtle.

For this tart I cook the pastry ahead because if the filling is cooked for too long it is inclined to spoil and dry up.

**SERVES 4 AS A MAIN COURSE,
6–8 AS A STARTER**

FOR THE PASTRY

225g/8oz flour

good pinch salt

1 teaspoon caster sugar

**175g/6oz unsalted butter or half
  butter and half pastry
  shortening, cubed**

1 egg yolk

1–2 tablespoons water

a little egg white

FOR THE FILLING

250g/9oz fresh spinach

200g/7oz waxy potatoes

1 tablespoon oil

**1/2 medium onion, peeled and
  chopped**

1 clove garlic, peeled and chopped

**1/4–1/2 red chilli, seeded and finely
  chopped (optional)**

1–2 teaspoons garam masala

125ml/4fl oz plain yoghurt

2 eggs

50g/1³/₄oz pinenuts

Start by making the pastry either by hand or, as here, in a food processor. Put the flour, salt and sugar into the bowl and process for a few seconds to mix and aerate them. Add the cubed butter and shortening, if using, and process until you have breadcrumbs. Add the egg yolk and 1 tablespoon of very cold water and process until the pastry comes together in a ball, adding a little more water if necessary. Take the pastry from the machine, roll it into a neat ball, wrap it in cling film and refrigerate it for 1/2 hour. Roll out the cold pastry and use it to line a 23-25cm/9-10in quiche tin. Prick the bottom lightly with the tines of a fork and return the prepared pastry case to the fridge for 1/2 hour.

◆ Heat the oven to 200°C/400°F/gas 6. Line the pastry case with a piece of foil and weight it down with baking beans, dried beans or uncooked rice. Bake for 15 minutes or until the pastry has just set then remove the beans and foil and return to the oven. Lower the temperature to 180°C/350°F/gas 4 and bake for a further 15 minutes or until the pastry is a light golden brown. Remove from the oven and seal the base by brushing it over with a little lightly beaten egg white.

◆ Wash and pick over the spinach, discarding any tough stalks. Put the wet spinach into a pan and cook until tender. Drain and leave until cool. Peel and dice the potatoes and cook in boiling salted water until tender. Heat the oil, sauté the onion, garlic and chilli, if using, until soft, then stir in the garam masala and cook to blend it in for a few more minutes.

◆ Squeeze the liquid from the spinach and put the leaves into a food processor and reduce to a purée. Turn the mixture into a bowl and stir in the potato, the onion mixture, the yoghurt and finally the eggs. Season to taste and spoon into the prepared pastry case. Lightly brown the pinenuts in a frying pan or under the grill and sprinkle them over the tart. Leave until cold.

TO FREEZE **Wrap in a plastic bag.**
TO DEFROST **Leave for 5–6 hours on the side or in the fridge for at least 14 hours.**
TO MICROWAVE **Not suitable.**
TO REHEAT **Cover the tart with foil. Heat the oven to 180°C/350°F/gas 4 and cook the tart until warm throughout, about 25–30 minutes or a little longer if the tart was not completely defrosted.**

❄ PANCAKE CAKE ⱽ

It is fun to produce a multi-storey pancake cake – and slightly less fiddly than rolling up individual pancakes. This in another of those dishes that doubles as a first course or a vegetarian main dish.

Pancakes take a little time to make but you could always prepare them in advance and store them in the freezer. The fillings are both quite easy.

**SERVES 4 AS A MAIN COURSE,
6 AS A STARTER**

FOR THE PANCAKES

150g/5½oz flour

2 eggs

1 tablespoon sunflower oil

400ml/14fl oz milk

butter for greasing

FOR THE BECHAMEL

50g/1¾oz butter

50g/1¾oz flour

300ml/10fl oz milk

150ml/5fl oz single cream

FOR THE SPINACH FILLING

250g/9oz spinach

40g/1½oz parmesan, grated

scraping nutmeg

FOR THE TOMATO FILLING

400g/14oz can chopped tomatoes

2 tablespoons olive oil

1 teaspoon sugar

1 clove garlic, peeled and finely
    chopped

50g/1¾oz butter

TO COOK

a little butter

Make the pancakes in a 25cm/10in pan following the instructions for Asparagus-Filled Pancakes (page 30). You should end up with 12, or at least 10 pancakes. Leave them, covered, in the fridge until needed. If you have pancakes in the freezer, take them out to defrost 2 hours beforehand.

◆ Next make the bechamel sauce by melting the butter, stirring in the flour and then slowly adding the milk then the cream. Bring to the boil and let it bubble, stirring from time to time, for 5 minutes then take from the hob and season. The sauce will be very thick.

◆ Wash the spinach and discard any tough stalks. The easiest option is to cook it in a microwave. Otherwise stuff all the wet leaves into a pan and cook over a high flame, turning from time to time until wilted. Leave until cool then squeeze out as much water as you can. Purée the spinach in a food processor, add half the bechamel and half the parmesan and season with salt, pepper and a little nutmeg.

◆ Tip the tomatoes into a pan, add the oil, sugar and garlic and simmer for 20 minutes. As it reduces, stir fairly frequently to stop the mix sticking to the bottom and burning. Turn the tomatoes into the rinsed-out food processor, add the remaining bechamel and quickly whizz it in. Season.

◆ Once the fillings are cool, you are ready to assemble the cake. Take 2 large sheets of foil and lay them crosswise on your work-top. Place a pancake in the middle and spread with a generous spoonful of the spinach mixture. Cover with another pancake and a spoonful of the tomato mixture. Repeat this with alternate sauces until everything is used up, ending with a pancake. Melt the 50g/1¾oz butter and brush it over the top and sides of the 'mountain' then sprinkle on the remaining parmesan. Bring up the opposite sides of the foil and fold them to seal, then do the same with the other piece.

TO FREEZE **Place flat in the freezer.**

TO DEFROST **Unwrap the cake, put into a greased ovenproof serving dish and leave for 6–7 hours on the side or for up to 24 hours in the fridge.**

TO MICROWAVE **Not suitable.**

TO COOK **Drizzle a little more melted butter over the top, cover lightly with foil and cook at 190°C/375°F/gas 5 for 35–40 minutes. Remove the foil for the last 10 minutes to give everything a chance to brown and bubble.**

vegetables

The recipes in this chapter are for the preparation of complete vegetable dishes and most of them, after defrosting, need no more than reheating in the oven or in a bain-marie. They are especially useful for those days when you have very little time for last-minute cooking. I give several ideas for vegetable purées which, particularly, make a very good accompaniment to any casserole or dish that contains gravy. I also give some simple recipes for braised vegetables and a couple of recipes for gratins, both of which can have cheese and/or ham added to turn them into light main-course dishes. I am not suggesting that fresh vegetables should be forgotten and as I like to produce two different vegetables at a meal I often serve a freshly cooked green vegetable as well as one of these from the freezer.

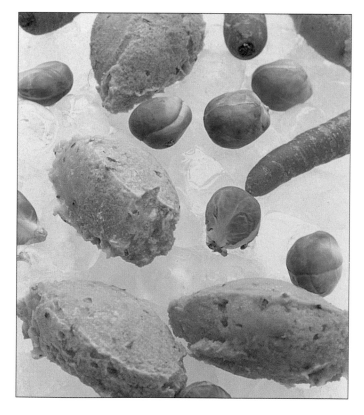

❄ VEGETABLE PUREES ^ᵛ

Mashed potatoes have always been a great favourite but mashed or puréed vegetables were really discovered with the advent of nouvelle cuisine and the timely arrival of the food processor. These purées have now established themselves as being more than a passing fancy and have shrugged off the image of baby food. All root vegetables and some green ones, such as brussels sprouts, purée well and can be interestingly varied by combining two or even three different vegetables together. Mashed potatoes are inclined to lose their texture in the freezer but mix them with another vegetable, such as celeriac, and they are fine.

Here are a few short recipes and ideas for puréed vegetables, having tried out some of these you should be able to mix and match and come up with ideas of your own. Puréed vegetables are quick to do with a food processor or blender and freeze and reheat very well indeed. The recipes should all serve 6.

❄ CARROT PUREE ^ᵛ

Carrots make a good and very versatile purée that can be flavoured to suit the occasion and to preserve their flavour I like to cook them vichy style - slowly in butter and a little water. (Carrots cooked like this are equally good frozen as they are, then defrosted and slowly reheated.)

The main recipe below is for a straight carrot purée, and very good it is too, but carrots take up other flavourings beautifully. To give you one or two ideas: cook a clove of garlic with the carrots and snip a bunch of chives into the purée; or, add garlic, some grated ginger and chopped coriander. The purée is also good swirled together with an equal quantity of mashed potato.

1kg/2lb 4oz carrots
50g/2oz butter
1 teaspoon sugar
3 tablespoons cream
bunch flat-leaf parsley, chopped

Peel the carrots and quarter them lengthwise. If the centre is hard cut it out and discard, and slice them thinly. Melt the butter in a wide heavy-based pan, add the carrots, sugar and seasoning and just enough water to cover. Bring to the boil and let it bubble fairly hard, reducing the heat if the liquid seems to be evaporating before the carrots are cooked. You should finish up with beautifully soft carrots bathed in a small amount of shiny glaze.

◆ Pour the contents of the pan into a food processor or blender and reduce to a purée. Check the seasoning add the cream and parsley and process to mix them in.

TO FREEZE **Spoon the purée into a rigid freezer box.**
TO DEFROST **Leave overnight in the fridge or for 5–6 hours on the side.**
TO MICROWAVE **Reheat according to your microwave instructions.**
TO REHEAT **Either put the purée into a dish, cover it well and heat for 30–40 minutes in the oven set at 160°C/325°F/gas 3 or put it into a bowl over a pan of simmering water and stir occasionally for 20 minutes or until hot.**

❄ CELERIAC PUREE ⱽ

Celeriac on its own makes a good purée with a rather stronger taste than when it is combined with potato (see overleaf).

4 tablespoons olive oil

2 shallots, peeled and chopped

1 large celeriac, peeled and cubed

2 sprigs thyme or ¹/₂ teaspoon dried thyme

approx 250ml/9fl oz light vegetable or chicken stock

Heat the olive oil and cook the shallots until soft. Add the celeriac cubes and sauté them for 1-2 minutes before adding the thyme and stirring in about three-quarters of the stock. Bring to the boil and let it simmer, adding more stock as necessary, until the celeriac is tender and the stock has nearly all been absorbed. Drain if necessary and reduce to a purée in a food processor. Season to taste.

TO FREEZE, TO DEFROST, TO MICROWAVE AND TO REHEAT
Follow the instructions for the Carrot Purée (opposite).

❄ CARROT AND PARSNIP RIPPLE ⱽ

The ripple effect can be conserved after freezing so long as you do not stir the purée again. (See photograph on page 123.)

500g/1lb 2oz carrots, peeled and sliced

500g/1lb 2oz parsnips, peeled and sliced

small bunch spring onions, trimmed and chopped

TO FINISH

1–2 teaspoons toasted sesame seeds

Cook the carrots in boiling water and purée them following the instructions opposite. Separately, boil the parsnips, drain, purée, then mix them with the spring onions.

◆ Spoon the two purées carefully, keeping them separate, into a freezer- and ovenproof dish. Stir together lightly to create an attractive ripple effect.

TO FREEZE, TO DEFROST, TO MICROWAVE AND TO REHEAT
Follow the instructions for the Carrot Purée (opposite).

❄ PUREE OF BRUSSELS SPROUTS ⱽ

This purée can be made with all sprouts or, for a mellower flavour, add some potatoes. It is also good flavoured with cumin rather than nutmeg or at Christmas time you could stir in a few chopped chestnuts. (See photograph on page 123.)

900g/2lb brussels sprouts

75g/2³/₄oz butter

50ml/2fl oz cream or milk

pinch nutmeg, grated

Trim the sprouts and cook until tender. Purée in a food processor then add the butter and cream or milk, season to taste, and process to mix them in.

TO FREEZE, TO DEFROST, TO MICROWAVE AND TO REHEAT
Follow the instructions for the Carrot Purée (opposite).

❋ FENNEL PUREE ⱽ

Rather than mix fennel with potato I take a tip from Sophie Grigson's book *Eat Your Greens* and mix it with a thick bechamel sauce. You can, if you want to cut down on the fat content, leave out the cream and make it entirely with milk.

6 fennel bulbs

25g/1oz butter

25g/1oz flour

75ml/2¹/₂fl oz milk

100ml/3¹/₂fl oz single cream

2 tablespoons flat-leaf parsley, chopped

TO REHEAT

2 tablespoons parmesan, grated (optional)

Cut the bottoms from the fennel bulbs and remove and discard any tough outside bits and stalks. Cube the bulbs and cook them in boiling salted water for 15-20 minutes or until tender. Meanwhile melt the butter, stir in the flour and then gradually add the milk and the cream to make a very thick bechamel sauce.

◆ Drain the cooked fennel then purée it in a food processor. Add the bechamel, parsley and seasoning and whizz them in.

◆ Spoon the purée into a shallow freezer- and ovenproof dish.

TO FREEZE **Cover with foil or a double layer of cling film.**

TO DEFROST **Leave on the side for 5–6 hours or overnight in the fridge.**

TO MICROWAVE **Follow the instructions for your oven to defrost and reheat, adding parmesan as below.**

TO REHEAT **If using, sprinkle on the parmesan. Put the foil-covered dish in the oven at 180°C/350°F/gas 4 for 30 minutes.**

❋ CELERIAC AND POTATO PUREE ⱽ

A good combination and one that can be jazzed up to give an interesting taste by adding a small squash. (See photograph opposite.)

750g/1lb 10oz floury potatoes

750g/1lb 10oz celeriac

small squash (optional)

75g/2³/₄oz butter

75ml/2¹/₂fl oz double cream or crème fraîche

75ml/2¹/₂fl oz milk

Peel the potatoes, cut them into chunks and cook in salted water until soft. Peel the celeriac, cut it into chunks and cook in salted water until soft.

◆ Peel and deseed a small squash, if using, and boil until tender.

◆ Put the vegetables into the food processor and reduce to a purée. Add the butter, cream, milk and some seasoning and briefly turn on the machine to blend all the ingredients together. If the purée is still rather stiff add a little more milk.

TO FREEZE, TO DEFROST, TO MICROWAVE AND TO REHEAT **Follow the instructions for the Carrot Purée (page 120).**

CELERIAC AND POTATO PUREE,
CARROT AND PARSNIP RIPPLE AND
PUREE OF BRUSSEL SPROUTS (PAGE 121)

❄ DUCHESSE POTATOES ⱽ

Potatoes in general do not freeze well as they are inclined to go watery and lose their texture. Mashed potato on its own is no exception but once it has egg yolk to hold it together it is fine and these duchesse potatoes freeze beautifully. The mixture is best if it is piped in swirls onto a baking sheet – one that will fit into your freezer.

SERVES 6

600g/1lb 5oz floury potatoes, peeled

50g/1³/₄oz butter

2 egg yolks

small pinch cayenne

Cube the potatoes and cook in boiling salted water until soft. Drain, then return the potatoes to the pan and dry them off over a low heat. Stir to stop them browning or burning at the edges.

◆ Put the dried potatoes through a mouli or mash them well then stir in the butter and egg yolks and season with salt, pepper and a small pinch of cayenne.

◆ Use a large plain or serrated nozzle to pipe the mixture into pyramid-shaped swirls onto a greased baking tray.

TO FREEZE **Freeze then cover with a double layer of cling film.**

TO DEFROST **Best cooked from frozen.**

TO MICROWAVE **Not suitable.**

TO REHEAT **Heat the oven to 200°C/400°F/gas 6, put in the tray and bake for 30–35 minutes or until the potatoes are browned round the edges.**

❄ PIQUANT RED CABBAGE ⱽ

Red cabbage takes a lot of cooking and is at its best when slowly stewed with spices and vinegar. It is very difficult to overcook and makes a perfect candidate for the freezer since it tastes better on reheating. It makes a warming and colourful accompaniment to winter casseroles, especially those based on game (see photograph on page 79). The raspberry vinegar cuts out any harshness and gives the cabbage a nice smooth flavour.

SERVES 6–8

1 medium red cabbage

75g/2³/₄oz butter

1 large onion, peeled and sliced

100ml/3¹/₂fl oz red wine

2 golden delicious apples

3 tablespoons raspberry vinegar

1 tablespoon demerara sugar

¹/₄ teaspoon ground nutmeg

¹/₄ teaspoon ground cinnamon

¹/₄ teaspoon ground cloves

Quarter the cabbage and chop out and discard the stem and any coarse outer leaves. Slice the cabbage either in a food processor or by hand and wash it in a bowl of cold water.

◆ Melt the butter in a good-sized pan, add in the onion and the drained, but still wet, cabbage. Stir in the wine, bring everything to the boil and stew over a very low heat or, better, put the pan into the oven at 150°C/300°F/gas 2 for 1-1¹/₂ hours or until the cabbage is tender.

◆ Peel and core the apples and cut them into cubes. Return the pan to the hob, add the apples, vinegar, sugar, spices and seasoning and bring back to the boil. Stir well and simmer for 5 minutes then take from the heat and leave until cold.

TO FREEZE **Pack into rigid freezer containers.**

TO DEFROST **Leave for 7–8 hours on the side or in the fridge for 18 hours or more.**

TO MICROWAVE **Follow your microwave instructions to defrost and reheat the red cabbage.**

TO REHEAT **Return the defrosted red cabbage to an ovenproof serving dish. If it looks a little dry sprinkle on a spoonful of so of water and reheat in the oven at 160°C/325°F/gas 3 for 45 minutes to 1 hour.**

❄ GRATIN OF FENNEL AND LEEKS ᵛ

As well as being a lovely crisp salad ingredient, fennel cooks well, but its flavour is assertive and it can be overpowering. Therefore I usually combine it with another vegetable and a sauce. I first came across this particular pairing in Alice Waters' book, *Chez Panisse Vegetables*, and it's a winner. The two vegetables complement each other beautifully and the fennel flavour becomes subtle rather than dominant. It is also a versatile dish and can be used, with or without a light dusting of parmesan, to accompany a main course or it can be sprinkled generously with the cheese and served as a first course or a vegetarian main course. (See photograph on page 99.)

SERVES 6 AS A VEGETABLE
ACCOMPANIMENT, 4 AS A
MAIN COURSE

3 large or 4 medium fennel bulbs

100g/3¹/₂oz butter

3 medium leeks

bunch parsley, chopped

40g/1¹/₂oz flour

450ml/16fl oz milk

parmesan, grated (optional)

Cut the tops and bottoms off the fennel bulbs then split each one in half lengthwise. Lay the halves flat on a board and cut into cubes. Melt 40g/1¹/₂oz of the butter in a sauté pan, add the fennel and cook gently for around 20 minutes or until tender.

◆ Meanwhile cut and discard the dark green tops from the leeks and, leaving the bottom 3cm/1¹/₄in intact, split them lengthwise. Wash them thoroughly in a large bowl then chop into half rounds.

◆ Remove the fennel from the pan wth a slotted spoon and put into a large bowl. Melt a further 20g/³/₄oz butter in the pan, add the leeks and cook them until very tender, which will take 10-15 minutes. Add them and the parsley to the fennel, season lightly and stir to mix.

◆ Melt the remaining 40g/1¹/₂oz butter in the pan, stir in the flour and cook gently for 2 minutes. Slowly, stirring all the time, add the milk and bring the sauce to the boil. Let it simmer for 3-4 minutes and season.

◆ Spoon the vegetables into a shallow freezer- and ovenproof dish and pour over the sauce. If liked, sprinkle lightly with a little cheese, or more heavily if the dish is to be a course on its own.

TO FREEZE **Cover the dish very tightly with foil.**

TO DEFROST **Leave on the side for 4–5 hours or overnight in the fridge.**

TO MICROWAVE **Not suitable.**

TO REHEAT **Put the dish into a pre-heated oven, 180°C/350°F/gas 4, for 30 minutes or until it is bubbling and the top is lightly browned.**

❄ BRAISED CELERY ᵛ

Braised celery is eaten a great deal in France and is the perfect accompaniment for French country casseroles. In recent years braised celery has been smartened up with the addition of dried mushrooms, unusual herbs or lashings of cream, but I still think it is nicest plain and simple. Supermarkets sell packets of celery hearts which are ideal for this recipe. You can make the dish more substantial by sprinkling it, before freezing, with breadcrumbs mixed with chopped walnuts.

SERVES 6

3–4 celery hearts, depending on size

2–3 carrots

25g/1oz butter plus extra for greasing the dish

25g/1oz flour

300ml/10fl oz strong vegetable or chicken stock

1 tablespoon sherry

Top and tail the celery hearts, cut off any leaves and peel any tough outside stalks. Peel the carrots and cut into slices. Liberally grease a shallow freezer- and ovenproof dish, lay the celery in it and distribute the carrot slices.

◆ Melt the butter, stir in the flour and cook, stirring, until the roux turns to a light brown. Pour in the stock and stir until you have a smooth sauce. Stir in the sherry, season and then pour over the celery.

◆ Cover the dish with foil and cook in the oven at 180°C/350°F/gas 4 for 30 minutes.

TO FREEZE **Leave the dish until cold then cover with foil or a double layer of cling-film.**

TO DEFROST **Leave on the side for 7–8 hours or in the fridge for up to 24 hours.**

TO MICROWAVE **Defrost and reheat according to your microwave instructions.**

TO REHEAT **Put the covered dish into the oven at 180°C/350°F/gas 4 for 30–40 minutes or until the celery is very tender and the sauce bubbling.**

❄ CARROTS AND PEAS WITH SAGE ᵛ

This makes a good and quite simple vegetable accompaniment. The assertive flavour of sage makes it a good partner for pork or other strong-flavoured meat. If you are going to serve this alongside a light or fish dish I would substitute another herb, perhaps thyme or tarragon. (See photograph on page 67.)

SERVES 6

400g/14oz small carrots, peeled

75g/2³/₄oz butter

2 medium red onions, peeled and roughly chopped

5–6 small sage leaves

2 teaspoons sugar

100ml/3¹/₂fl oz vegetable or light chicken stock

350g/12oz fresh shelled or frozen petits pois

Slice the carrots, but not too thinly. Melt the butter and stir in the onion, carrots and torn sage leaves, sprinkle on the sugar and season lightly.

◆ Cook for a few minutes before pouring in the stock. Cover and cook gently for 10 minutes then remove the lid and if you are using fresh peas add them now. Continue cooking for another 10 minutes or until the carrots are just soft and the stock has nearly all evaporated. If you are using frozen peas stir them in just before removing the pan from the heat. Leave until cold.

TO FREEZE **Turn into a rigid freezer container.**

TO DEFROST **Leave on the side for 6–7 hours or in the fridge for 15 hours.**

TO MICROWAVE **Follow your microwave instructions to reheat.**

TO REHEAT **Return to a pan, reheat over a low flame and serve immediately or the peas will overcook.**

❄ PARSNIP AND LEEK BAKE ᵛ

Another ever-useful dish that can be served as an accompanying vegetable, as a vegetarian main course, or with cheese, bacon or ham added to it as a first course.

I always like to spice up parsnip a little with curry powder, but take note of the dish that it is going to accompany before being heavy-handed with the spice. You may even prefer to leave it out altogether.

SERVES 6

750g/1lb 10oz parsnips, peeled

2–3 cloves garlic, peeled

½–2 teaspoons garam masala

2 tablespoons gruyère or parmesan, grated (optional)

2 tablespoons cooked bacon or ham, chopped (optional)

600g/1lb 5oz leeks

6 tablespoons olive oil

1 shallot

75g/2¾oz fresh breadcrumbs

Cut the parsnips into chunks, put into a pan of salted water and bring to the boil. After about 5 minutes add the garlic and continue to cook until the parsnip is tender. Drain and purée in a food processor or mash them. Season, add garam masala to taste and the cheese, bacon or ham if using.

◆ Wash the leeks well then slice them, and stew until tender in 3 tablespoons of the olive oil and a little water. Turn up the heat to let some of the water evaporate then drain them well.

◆ Spoon the leeks into a shallow freezer- and ovenproof dish and then spread the parsnip over the top.

◆ Peel and finely chop the shallot and sauté it in the remaining oil. When it is soft add the breadcrumbs and, stirring constantly, cook until golden. Spread the breadcrumbs over the top of the parsnip.

TO FREEZE **Cover the dish in foil or a double layer of cling film.**

TO DEFROST **Leave on the side for 7–8 hours or in the fridge for 18–20 hours.**

TO MICROWAVE **Follow your microwave instructions to defrost the dish. It is better cooked in a conventional oven.**

TO REHEAT **Set the oven to 180°C/350°F/gas 4 and heat the defrosted dish for 35–40 minutes, or slightly longer if it has not completely defrosted.**

❄ BRAISED CHICORY ᵛ

Braised chicory freezes well and makes a good accompanying vegetable. You can also turn it into a main course by wrapping the braised chicory heads in slices of ham and sprinkling them with parmesan. (See photograph on page 51.)

SERVES 6

6 heads chicory (red or white)

100g/3¹/₂oz butter

juice ¹/₂ lemon

1 teaspoon sugar

1 tablespoon balsamic vinegar

Cut the chicory heads in half lengthwise.

◆ Melt the butter in a large frying or sauté pan and turn the chicory in it. Fry gently for a few minutes, turning once or twice and when it starts to colour pour in 300ml/10fl oz water and add the lemon juice, sugar and some seasoning. Leave to bubble gently, still turning from time to time until soft.

◆ Use a slotted spoon to remove the chicory to a shallow freezer- and ovenproof dish. Add the balsamic vinegar to the sauce and leave it to simmer and reduce slightly until it is syrupy, then pour it over the chicory.

TO FREEZE **Cover the dish with foil or a double layer of cling film.**

TO DEFROST **Leave on the side for 4–5 hours or in the fridge overnight.**

TO MICROWAVE **Follow the instructions for your microwave to defrost and reheat.**

TO REHEAT **Put the foil-covered dish in the oven at 190°C/375°F/gas 5 for 25–30 minutes or until it is bubbling and flecked with brown.**

❄ BABY ONIONS IN A SWEET TOMATO SAUCE ᵛ

This is my version for the freezer of a Sicilian dish I found in a large and lovely book called *Italy the Beautiful Cookbook* by Lorenza de'Medici. The Sicilians are very partial to sweet and sour sauces and, like the Caponata di Melanzane on page 21, this is both sweetened and sharpened by the addition of sugar and vinegar. I have been quite restrained about the amounts and to bring out the various flavours I have used balsamic vinegar. If, however, you want to eat the onions as a starter you could sharpen the sauce with more vinegar.

Try to find pearl or baby white onions but if you can't use pickling onions.

SERVES 6

900g/2lb pearl or baby onions

50g/1³/₄oz raisins

2 tablespoons olive oil

400g/14oz can chopped tomatoes

1 clove

2 tablespoons red wine vinegar

1–2 teaspoons sugar

Cook the onions for 8 minutes in boiling water then drain and leave to cool a little. Put the raisins in a bowl, cover with water and leave to soak.

◆ Top, tail and peel the cooled onions. In a deep frying pan heat the oil, add the onions and cook, shaking them frequently until they are lightly browned. Add the tomatoes and the clove and cook, stirring occasionally, for 10 minutes then pour on the vinegar, stir in the drained raisins and sugar to taste. Remove the clove from the tomato sauce then season to taste.

TO FREEZE **Turn into a rigid freezer con- tainer or a gratin dish and cover well.**

TO DEFROST **Leave on the side for 4–5 hours or in the fridge for at least 15 hours.**

TO MICROWAVE **Follow your microwave instructions to defrost and reheat.**

TO REHEAT **Put the covered gratin dish in the oven set at 180°C/350°F/gas 4 and heat for ¹/₂ hour.**

❄ PARSNIP CHIPS ⱽ

Parsnips make delicious crisp and crunchy chips which, after preparation, freeze beautifully. They then simply need to be baked in the oven. I prefer to use small, quite young parsnips as large ones have a woody central core.

SERVES 6

1kg/2lb 4oz small parsnips, peeled

2 tablespoons flour, seasoned

1 teaspoon curry powder (optional)

TO COOK

3 tablespoons oil

Top and tail the parsnips and cut them crosswise into 5cm/2in lengths and then downwards into halves or quarters, and with the thick end cut down again to make chips.

◆ Bring a large pan of salted water to the boil, throw in the parsnips, bring back to the boil and cook for 2 minutes. Drain, and when they have dried a little sprinkle with the seasoned flour and, if desired, some curry powder. Toss the chips to cover them well with flour.

TO FREEZE **Put them into a freezer bag.**

TO DEFROST **Leave on the side for 1 hour or until you can separate the chips with a fork.**

TO MICROWAVE **Not suitable.**

TO COOK **Heat the oven to 200°C/ 400°F/gas 6. Spread out the chips on a baking tray, drizzle over the oil. Turn the parsnips until they are well covered with the oil. Cook until they are crisp and golden – about 35–40 minutes, turning them once or twice.**

❄ SWEETCORN FRITTERS ⱽ

These little fritters are good with chicken or pork dishes or can be served with a tomato sauce as a first course. You can have them plain or jazzed up with a little chilli or sun-dried tomato.

MAKES 12–18 FRITTERS, DEPENDING ON SIZE

2 eggs, separated

100g/3½oz flour

4 tablespoons milk

330g/11½oz can sweetcorn kernels

½ teaspoon chilli flakes (optional)

1 tablespoon chopped sun-dried tomato (optional)

3–4 tablespoons sunflower oil

Put the egg yolks and flour into a food processor, turn it on and slowly add the milk through the feed tube and mix until smooth. Pour it into a bowl, stir in the well-drained sweetcorn kernels and, if using, the chilli flakes or sun-dried tomato. Season the batter. Whisk the egg whites until stiff and fold them into the mixture.

◆ In a frying pan heat the oil then drop in the mixture, a dessert spoonful at a time. Flatten the fritters a little and fry until brown then turn them and fry the other side. Remove to a plate covered with a piece of kitchen paper.

TO FREEZE **Pack the fritters in freezer bags.**

TO DEFROST **Leave on a plate on the side for 1 hour.**

TO MICROWAVE **Not suitable.**

TO COOK **Heat a little oil in a frying pan and fry on both sides until the fritters are hot and crisp. Serve immediately.**

❄ BEETROOT AND JERUSALEM ARTICHOKE GRATIN ⓥ

Different but complementary flavours and colours make this dish so attractive. It also goes well with many other foods and is especially good served alongside a plain grilled fish fillet. Try it also with the Rabbit in Cider with Herbs and Dijon Mustard (page 81) or one of the pork dishes. You could always add some grated gruyère to the artichoke sauce and serve it as a first course or a main vegetarian dish.

SERVES 6

200g/7oz beetroot, cooked and peeled

375g/13oz Jerusalem artichokes

700ml/1¼ pints milk

bunch parsley

55g/2oz butter

40g/1½oz flour

3–4 tablespoons sour cream

1–2 tablespoons creamed horseradish

4 tablespoons parmesan, grated

3–4 tablespoons breadcrumbs

Cube the beetroot and reserve. Top, tail, peel and dice the artichokes and keep them on one side. It is a fiddly job and you will probably end up with around 200g/7oz of artichoke dice. Put the artichokes and 250ml/9fl oz of the milk, the stalks of the parsley (keep the leaves until needed) and some salt and pepper into a pan and slowly bring to the boil. Simmer, stirring occasionally for 15 minutes or until tender. Drain, discard the parsley stalks but reserve the milk.

◆ Melt 40g/1½oz of the butter, stir in the flour then slowly add the remaining milk. Stirring, bring to the boil and cook until you have a smooth, thick sauce. Pour half the sauce into a bowl, season and add the sour cream and horseradish to taste. Stir in the beetroot dice and if the sauce seems too thick add a little of the reserved milk. Spoon the mixture into a gratin or fairly shallow freezer- and ovenproof dish.

◆ Put the pan back onto the heat and stir in enough of the reserved milk to thin the sauce so that it runs off the spoon easily. Season, and stir in the chopped parsley leaves, half the parmesan and finally the artichoke dice. Use this mixture to cover the beetroot then sprinkle the top with the remaining parmesan and the breadcrumbs and dot with the remaining butter.

TO FREEZE **Cover the dish with foil or a double layer of clingfilm.**

TO DEFROST **Leave for 7–8 hours on the side or in the fridge for 16–18 hours.**

TO MICROWAVE **Follow your microwave instructions to defrost and reheat.**

TO REHEAT **Put the defrosted dish in the oven at 180°C/350°F/gas 4 for 30–35 minutes or until it is hot and the top has browned. You could cook it when partially defrosted, but it will need longer in the oven.**

desserts

Let me start by saying that I really enjoy desserts. There's something very satisfactory about ending a meal with an indulgence, and entertaining friends gives me the perfect excuse to fall for such an indulgence. Desserts and puddings by their very nature are seasonal. Many of them are made with fruit which has to be caught when it is at its ripe and juicy best, and when fresh fruit is scarce and the weather cold, it's nice to finish a meal with a more filling pudding which will send the guests on their way with a good glow in their tummies. To start off the section I give a recipe for Almond Tuiles. This may sound odd but biscuits stay fresh-tasting and crisp for longer when kept in a box in the freezer rather than stored in an airtight tin. They make a very good crunchy accompaniment to many desserts and are really useful to have to hand. For the same reason, I finish the book with a simple recipe for cheese straws which I and my family are very partial to, even though I am not sure why I bother to freeze them as they always seem to have disappeared within a day or so of being baked.

❄ ALMOND TUILES

These little curved almond biscuits are the ideal accompaniment to many puddings. They will keep for a few days in an airtight tin but they will keep far longer and stay crisper and fresher-tasting if they are frozen.

**MAKES 20–30 TUILES
DEPENDING ON SIZE**

60g/2¼oz unsalted butter

140g/5oz icing sugar

3 egg whites

100g/3½oz flour

1 teaspoon vanilla essence

25g/1oz flaked almonds

Melt the butter and leave it to cool. Sift the icing sugar into the egg whites and whisk together and when they are fully amalgamated sift in the flour and stir to incorporate it. Finally stir in the melted butter and vanilla essence. Leave in the fridge for 15 minutes and prepare the baking sheets.

◆ Heat the oven to 200°C/400°F/gas 6 and line two baking sheets with silicone paper.

◆ Spread a good spoonful of the mixture into circles on one of the baking sheets. You need to spread the mixture very thinly; not for nothing is it sometimes called stencil paste. Sprinkle some almonds over the top.

◆ Put the baking tray into the oven and start to prepare the other sheet, putting it into the oven when the first sheet comes out.

◆ After 5-8 minutes or when the biscuits are colouring all over and fairly dark brown round the edges take the tray from the oven. Immediately lift the biscuits off with a spatula and, to shape them, lay them over an oiled rolling pin and leave until hardened. Repeat when the second tray is cooked and continue until you have used up all the mixture.

TO FREEZE **Pack the cooled tuiles into a rigid freezer container.**

TO DEFROST **Leave on the side for ½ hour.**

TO MICROWAVE **Not suitable.**

TO FINISH **Add to any fruity pudding.**

❄ KUMQUAT BAVAROIS WITH A FLUFFY BASE

The elusive taste of kumquats makes this bavarois different and quite special. Being fruity and not too rich it would make a very suitable pudding for a Sunday lunch party when children are present.

Italian Savoiardi sponge fingers are made for puddings, tiramisu especially, and soften and soak up liquids beautifully. They are now sold in many supermarkets as well as delicatessens.

SERVES 6–8

a little butter for greasing

packet Savoiardi sponge fingers

450g/1lb kumquats

225g/8oz sugar

5 leaves gelatine

2 eggs, separated

25g/1oz sugar

1 teaspoon vanilla essence

150ml/5fl.oz double cream

TO FINISH

handful mint leaves (optional)

Liberally grease a charlotte mould or soufflé dish and line the bottom and sides with sponge fingers.

◆ Halve the kumquats and put them, the sugar and 300ml/10fl.oz water into a pan, bring to the boil and let it simmer for about $1/2$ hour. Drain off and reserve the liquid. Put the kumquats through a mouli or purée them in a food processor and then press through a sieve. Add the purée to the liquid. Soak 3 leaves of gelatine in cold water for 5 minutes. Heat a few tablespoons of the kumquat mixture, stir in the drained gelatine and, when it has dissolved, add it to the rest of the mixture.

◆ Pour a little of the mixture into the prepared mould. You need just enough to soak the biscuits in the base (any more and the biscuits will float to the surface). Keep the rest of the jelly mixture in a warm place and put the mould into the freezer or fridge to set the soaked base. When it has set, slowly add the remaining jelly and return to the fridge.

◆ Whisk the egg yolks, sugar and vanilla essence together. Heat the double cream and pour it, whisking all the time, onto the egg mixture. Pour into a saucepan and heat. Continue whisking and take from the heat before it boils or it will separate. Soak 2 gelatine leaves in water for 5 minutes, drain, then stir into the hot custard. Leave until cold and when it is on the point of setting whisk the egg whites until stiff and fold them in. Spoon onto the set jelly and cut any protruding sponge fingers level with the pudding.

TO FREEZE **Cover with foil or a double layer of cling film.**

TO DEFROST **Leave in the fridge for at least 12 hours.**

TO MICROWAVE **Not suitable.**

TO FINISH **Run a knife round the mould and turn the bavarois out onto a serving dish. Decorate, if liked, with some mint leaves and/or whipped cream.**

TO SERVE **Hand round a jug of cream.**

❄ STRAWBERRY CREAMS

These little strawberry creams are simplicity itself to make and are served, not quite as an ice cream, but still very cold. Don't be put off by the addition of balsamic vinegar; for some reason it does wonders for strawberries and brings out the true flavour of the fruit. Buy a few fresh strawberries on the day of your party to decorate the ramekins.

SERVES 6

500g/1lb 2oz strawberries

100g/3¹/₂oz icing sugar

1 teaspoon balsamic vinegar

150ml/5fl oz double cream

100g/3¹/₂oz crème fraîche

TO FINISH

1 punnet strawberries

Almond Tuiles (page 132) or biscuits

Purée the strawberries in a food processor then sieve to eliminate the pips. Whisk the icing sugar and vinegar into the puréed strawberries. Whip the double cream until very stiff then stir the crème fraîche into it. Whisk the cream into the strawberry mixture and taste; you may want to add a little more sugar.

TO FREEZE **Spoon into individual ramekins and cover with foil or a double layer of cling film.**

TO DEFROST **Remove from the freezer to the fridge about 1¹/₂ hours before serving.**

TO MICROWAVE **Not suitable.**

TO FINISH **Put a strawberry, sliced, onto each ramekin and serve with a biscuit or Almond Tuile on the side.**

❄ MERINGUES

It is usually recommended that meringues be stored in an airtight tin but try keeping them in the freezer instead. They need to be well wrapped in plastic bags or kept in plastic freezer boxes but they emerge crisp and very fresh-tasting and, wonder of wonders, they need no defrosting and can be eaten straight from the freezer.

SERVES 6

4 egg whites

200g/7oz caster sugar

1 teaspoon cornflour

¹/₂ teaspoon white wine vinegar

TO FINISH

2 punnets strawberries

150ml/5fl oz double cream

Line 2 baking sheets with greaseproof paper, and preheat the oven to 140°C/275°F/gas 1.

◆ To make the meringues whisk the egg whites until stiff, then whisk in the sugar, a little at a time. Add the cornflour and vinegar and continue whisking until it renders a glossy meringue consistency.

◆ Spoon generous dollops of the mixture onto the baking sheets, then bake in the oven for 1¹/₂ hours or until the meringues are crisp.

◆ Turn off the oven and leave the meringues to cool.

TO FREEZE **Wrap meringues in plastic bags or put in plastic freezer boxes.**

TO DEFROST **Eat from frozen.**

TO FINISH **Accompanied by strawberries and fresh cream, meringues are the ultimate instant pudding.**

❄ HAZELNUT AND MOCHA MERINGUE

This pudding is an old favourite, one might almost say a classic, but it has stood the test of time and every time I produce it the whole plateful disappears in a trice.

The cream is flavoured with coffee and dark brown muscovado sugar which is an old trick that brings out and enhances the flavour of the coffee.

SERVES 6–8

100g/3¹/₂oz hazelnuts

200g/7oz caster sugar

4 egg whites

1 teaspoon instant coffee

1 tablespoon dark muscovado sugar

300ml/10fl oz double cream

50g/1³/₄oz plain chocolate, grated

TO FINISH

2 tablespoons chocolate, grated

icing sugar

whipped cream (optional)

Start by making the meringue. Use a plate to mark out two circles of approximately 22cm/8¹/₂in diameter on sheets of silicone paper. Put the sheets flat onto two baking trays.

◆ If the hazelnuts need skinning place them on a baking tray and put them into a fairly hot oven or under a grill for 10 minutes then rub the skins off in a tea towel. Return them to the oven, or, if you have bought them ready skinned, put them into a hot oven to bake for about 10 minutes until golden brown. You'll need to turn them once or twice, and watch them carefully as the difference between a lovely shade of brown and burnt is about 5 seconds. Put the nuts and a tablespoon of the sugar into a food processor and grind down finely.

◆ Whisk the egg whites until stiff then whisk in the rest of the caster sugar, a little at a time. Continue whisking until you have a glossy meringue, then use a spoon to fold in the ground hazelnuts. Spoon onto the marked circles, spreading it to the edges and flattening it on the top. Bake at 140°C/275°F/gas 1 for 1¹/₄ hours, or until the meringue is crisp, then turn off the oven and leave the meringue in it until cold.

◆ To make the filling dissolve the coffee and the sugar in a tablespoon or so of very hot water. Whisk the cream until it is stiff, stir in the coffee syrup followed by the grated chocolate and then spread it over one of the meringue discs. Place the other disc on top, flat side down, but don't press down too hard or the cream will ooze out at the edge.

TO FREEZE Leave the completed cake on a plate and freeze. When it is fully frozen carefully wrap it in cling film or foil and return to the freezer.

TO DEFROST Leave on the side for 4–5 hours or in the fridge for at least 15–16 hours.

TO FINISH Sprinkle with the chocolate and, to add colour, sift a little icing sugar over the top and, if liked, hand round a bowl of whipped cream.

❄ RHUBARB AND GINGER STRUDEL

Warm strudel with lots of crispy pastry wrapped round a fruity filling is a very welcome dessert on long dark winter days and this one, made with delicate pink forced rhubarb, also brings to mind the thought that spring is on the way.

The size of the filo sheets dictates the size of the strudel and the ones I have used are the most easily available size, enough only for 4 people. Make two strudels if you are feeding 6 and any leftovers can be eaten cold.

SERVES 4

350g/12oz forced rhubarb

1 orange

4 tablespoons golden syrup

1 tablespoon ginger syrup from the stem ginger jar

100g/3^1/$_2$oz white bread, without crusts

75g/2^3/$_4$oz granulated sugar

40g/1^1/$_2$oz butter

6 sheets (8 x 32cm/3^1/$_4$ x 12^1/$_2$in) filo pastry, defrosted

2 knobs stem ginger, chopped

Top and tail the rhubarb, remove any stringy skin and cut into 2-3cm/^{3}/$_4$-1^1/$_4$in lengths. Zest and juice the orange. Put the orange juice, golden syrup and stem ginger syrup into a small saucepan and heat slightly. Add the rhubarb, turn it in the syrup then put it back on the heat and, stirring from time to time, bring slowly to the boil. Simmer, stirring once or twice, for 2 minutes then remove from the heat and immerse as much of the fruit as you can in the liquid. Cover the pan and and leave until cold.

◆ Reduce the bread to crumbs in a food processor, then add the sugar and process them together. Drain the rhubarb, reserving the syrup, and leave the fruit to dry. Melt the butter.

◆ Cover the worktop with a dry tea towel. Keeping the filo pastry covered by a dampened tea towel at all times, proceed to lay out the sheets, semi-staggered. Put the first sheet down on the dry tea towel and brush it all over with melted butter. Sprinkle on around a quarter of the breadcrumb mixture, then cover it with the second sheet placed about 2.5cm/1in down from the top. Butter and breadcrumb it and put on the third sheet up 2.5cm/1in to cover the area of the first sheet. Repeat with the fourth sheet covering the second one and the fifth covering the first and third ones. Butter the top sheet but don't sprinkle it with breadcrumbs.

◆ Lay the rhubarb onto the pastry, leaving a margin of 2cm/1in all round. Sprinkle the ginger over the rhubarb. Turn the short top and bottom ends up over the rhubarb and then using the towel roll it up into a sausage with the long sides meeting in the middle. I now find it easiest to cheat a little and to butter another sheet of pastry, fold it in half lengthwise and, after brushing the seam on the strudel with butter, to neaten and seal it with the extra sheet.

◆ Pour the reserved syrup into a pan and boil until it has reduced and become more syrupy. In a bowl mix the cornflour with a couple of spoonfuls of the syrup then return it to the pan and, stirring constantly, let it thicken. Take from the heat and leave to cool.

TO FREEZE Carefully, using the tea towel to help you, wrap the strudel in cling film and transfer it to the freezer. (Or you could put it in the freezer wrapped in the tea towel and then when it is frozen wrap it in cling film.) Freeze the syrup separately in a rigid container.

TO DEFROST The strudel is best cooked from frozen but take the syrup from the freezer and leave on the side for a couple of hours.

TO MICROWAVE Not suitable.

TO COOK Heat the oven to 190°C/ 375°F/gas 5. Put the frozen strudel onto a baking sheet and bake for 30 minutes or until crisp and golden. Turn off the oven and leave to cool for about 10 minutes. Heat the syrup and serve it alongside the warm strudel.

TO SERVE Hand round crème fraîche or double cream.

❄ ICED ORANGE SOUFFLES

Soufflé isn't strictly the correct term but the alternatives were the equally incorrect ice cream or semi-freddo. Anyway the name is really only there for identification – it's the look and taste that matter.

The orange juice is boiled and reduced by at least half its volume. This gives a very concentrated flavour and little liquid to add to the mixture which might, in larger amounts, crystallise when frozen.

Either fill individual ramekins or serve it from a large soufflé dish, with or without a paper collar.

SERVES 6

zest 1 orange

1 tablespoon Grand Marnier or other orange-based liqueur

300ml/10fl oz fresh orange juice (juice 2–3 large oranges)

juice ½ lemon

150g/5½oz granulated sugar

2 egg whites

300ml/10fl oz whipping cream

Soak the orange zest in the Grand Marnier and leave on one side. In a small but wide pan bring the orange and lemon juices to the boil and bubble for around 10 minutes or until reduced by half to two-thirds. Add the sugar, stir until dissolved, then bring back to the boil and bubble until you have a syrup, but be careful not to let it burn and caramelise.

◆ While it is boiling, use an electric whisk to beat the egg whites until stiff. Pour in the hot orange syrup while continuing to whisk. Plunge the bowl into a larger one containing cold water and keep whisking until the mixture is cold and has thickened so that the trail of the whisk is left on the surface of the meringue.

◆ Wash the beaters and whisk the cream until it holds soft peaks. Stir the orange zest and Grand Marnier into the mixture then fold in the meringue. Spoon into ramekins or a large soufflé dish.

TO FREEZE **Put the soufflé, uncovered, in the freezer. When frozen, cover with foil or a double layer of cling film.**

TO DEFROST **Eat as a semi-freddo.**

TO MICROWAVE **Not suitable.**

TO FINISH **Transfer from freezer to fridge 15–20 minutes before serving for ramekins and up to 1 hour for a large soufflé dish. Remove the covers and any collars.**

ICED PRALINE SOUFFLE (PAGE 140); BOTTOM:

ICED ORANGE SOUFFLE

❄ ICED PRALINE SOUFFLES

I always think of praline as being very magical. No conjuror could do better than the cook and turn a few nuts and spoonfuls of sugar into such a lovely crunchy caramelly mixture.

These little iced soufflés make a light and delicious pudding and 'iced' is the important word. They should be served very, very cold, as semi-freddos, so do trust the time I suggest for transferring them from freezer to fridge. Left for much longer they become floppy and soft and lose a lot of their impact.

The soufflés look very impressive if you tie a collar of silicone or greaseproof paper round each ramekin and fill both the ramekin and collar with the soufflé. The collar is then removed on taking the soufflés from the freezer to show very professional-looking wobbly tops. But if you are short of time, or want to make 8 rather then 6 soufflés, just fill the ramekins to the top. (See photograph on page 139.)

MAKES 6–8 SOUFFLES

FOR THE PRALINE
100g/3¹/₂oz unskinned almonds
100g/3¹/₂oz granulated sugar

FOR THE SOUFFLES
4 eggs, separated
75g/2³/₄oz caster sugar
300ml/10fl oz whipping cream

TO FINISH
25g/1oz praline

Lightly brown the almonds in the oven or under the grill.

◆ Put the sugar and 3 tablespoons of water into a small pan and melt the sugar over a low heat. Bring to boiling point and boil fast until you have a golden caramel. Add the almonds and stir over a moderate heat for the caramel to darken slightly. Quickly pour the bubbling hot mixture onto a piece of oiled foil and leave until cold.

◆ Break into pieces and pulverise in a food processor, or crush the praline between sheets of greaseproof paper with a rolling pin. Store in an airtight container for 2 or 3 weeks or use immediately.

◆ Put the egg yolks and sugar into a bowl and use an electric whisk to beat until the mixture has trebled in volume, then stir in 75g/2³/₄oz praline. In separate basins, whisk the cream then the egg whites until stiff. Fold the egg whites into the praline mixture then gently stir in the cream. Spoon into the ramekins.

TO FREEZE **Put the ramekins, uncovered, into the freezer. When they are frozen, cover each one with foil or a double layer of cling film.**
TO DEFROST **Eat as a semi-freddo.**
TO MICROWAVE **Not suitable.**
TO FINISH **About ¹/₂ hour before eating the soufflés, transfer them from the freezer to the fridge and remove the covers and collars if you used them. Sprinkle each one with the leftover praline.**

❄ APPLE, ALMOND AND RAISIN CRUMBLE

Forget nursery food, apple crumble can be a truly delicious pudding so do give this one, which is full of raisins, almonds, orange and spices, a try. I have also, rather like a French apple tart, given the apple a bit of body by making a base of cooked-down bramley apples and then adding some cubed golden delicious apples.

SERVES 8

1 orange

75g/2³/₄oz raisins

2 bramley apples – about 600g/1lb 5oz

50g/1³/₄oz granulated sugar

125g/4¹/₂oz firm butter

3 golden delicious apples – about 400g/14oz

75g/2³/₄oz ground almonds

75g/2³/₄oz plain white flour

75g/2³/₄oz demerara sugar

75g/2³/₄oz rolled oats

50g/1³/₄oz flaked almonds

¹/₄ teaspoon ground cloves

¹/₄ teaspoon ground cinnamon

¹/₄ teaspoon nutmeg

Preferably 2–3 hours before you make the pudding, zest the orange and keep it on one side. Squeeze out the juice and put the raisins to soak in it.

◆ Peel and core the bramley apples, cut them into chunks and put them into a pan with the granulated sugar, 50g/1³/₄oz of the butter and 150ml/5fl oz water. Cook, stirring fairly often, until the apples have broken down into a purée then remove from the heat.

◆ Drain and keep the raisins and stir the orange juice into the purée. Peel and core the golden delicious apples, cut into bite-sized chunks and stir them into the apple mixture. Transfer the mixture to a freezer- and ovenproof dish – a lasagne dish is perfect.

◆ In a large bowl mix together the raisins, ground almonds, flour, demerara sugar, rolled oats, flaked almonds, orange zest and spices. Chop the remaining butter into the mixture and use your fingers to rub it in until it resembles breadcrumbs. Sprinkle this mixture evenly over the top of the apple.

TO FREEZE Cover well with foil or a double layer of cling film.

TO DEFROST Leave on the side for 8–9 hours or in the fridge for at least 18 hours.

TO MICROWAVE Not suitable.

TO REHEAT Heat at 180°C/350°F/gas 4 for 35–40 minutes or until the top is bubbling and golden.

TO SERVE Hand round a jug of cream or, for real treats, a bowl of clotted cream.

❄ VANILLA CHEESECAKE WITH CHOCOLATE AND AMARETTI

Cooked cheesecake is well known to freeze beautifully and this also tastes sublime. The base is made with chocolate amaretti and the centre is a lovely velvety smooth mixture of mascarpone and curd cheese flavoured with lots of vanilla. The topping, made of cocoa and sugar, is then covered with a layer of sour cream.

Do use genuine vanilla essence, not vanilla flavouring. I have been vague about the amount of essence as every bottle seems to vary in strength. I would just add, don't be too cautious. If you prefer you could use strong-flavoured vanilla sugar or add the seeds from a vanilla pod to the cheese mixture.

SERVES 6–8

225g/8oz chocolate amaretti biscuits or 225g/8oz plain amaretti and 1 tablespoon cocoa powder

75g/2³/₄oz butter

250g/9oz mascarpone

250g/9oz curd cheese

100g/3¹/₂oz caster sugar

3 eggs, separated

1 tablespoon plain flour

2–3 teaspoons vanilla essence

1 tablespoon cocoa powder mixed with 1 tablespoon caster sugar

150ml/5fl oz sour cream

TO FINISH

1 teaspoon cocoa powder

1 teaspoon icing sugar

You will need an 22cm/8¹/₂in cake tin with a removable base and preferably with a spring clip side. Grease the tin well and line the bottom with silicone paper.

◆ To prepare the base, crush the amaretti in a food processor or put them in a bag and bash it with a rolling pin. Melt the butter and add the biscuits, and the cocoa, if used. Mix well together. Turn the mixture into the prepared tin and spread it evenly over the bottom, patting it down with the back of a spoon.

◆ In a food processor or using a large fork, combine the cheeses well then add the sugar, egg yolks, flour and vanilla essence to taste. Whisk the egg whites until stiff and gently fold in the cheese mixture. Turn it into the cake tin.

◆ Sprinkle the cocoa powder and sugar mixture over the top of the cheesecake using a small sieve. Cover with foil and bake at 160°C/325°F/gas 3 for 1 hour. Take from the oven and drizzle the sour cream over the top using a spoon to spread it evenly, then leave until cold.

TO FREEZE Remove the cake from the tin, but leave it on the metal base and freeze. When it is frozen wrap it well in foil or a double layer of cling film.

TO DEFROST **Take the cheesecake from the freezer and immediately remove the metal base and silicone paper. Put it, uncovered, onto a serving plate. Leave to defrost in the fridge for at least 10 hours.**

TO MICROWAVE **Nor suitable.**

TO FINISH **Serve cold from the fridge sprinkled with the cocoa and icing sugar mixed together.**

❄ CHOCOLATE AND AMARETTI MOUSSES

The method for this mousse is unusual in that the sugar is boiled with water to make a syrup which is then beaten into the egg whites. This Italian-style meringue is then folded into the chocolate, butter and egg yolk mixture and spooned into ramekins which contain an amaretto soaked in brandy. The result is a mousse with marvellous texture and taste. I like to make individual ones and serve as semi-freddos, defrosted for no more than 10 minutes.

SERVES 6

9 amaretti biscuits

12 teaspoons brandy

100g/3¹/₂oz good quality bitter chocolate

50g/1³/₄oz butter

2 eggs, separated

100g/3¹/₂oz sugar

Put an amaretto each into the bottom of six ramekins and sprinkle with brandy. The amount you use is up to you but I like to put in up to 2 teaspoons in each which is enough to soak into the biscuits and soften them throughout.

◆ Melt the chocolate and butter, either in a basin over a pan of hot water or in your microwave. Stir the chocolate and butter until they have amalgamated then leave to cool a little before whisking in the egg yolks. Leave on one side.

◆ Put the sugar in a pan with 5 tablespoons water over a low heat. Stir occasionally until the sugar has melted. Bring the sugar mixture to the boil and simmer for 1-1¹/₂ minutes while you whisk the egg whites until stiff. Keep a careful eye on the sugar syrup and if it shows any sign of caramelising remove it from the heat immediately. Whisking all the time, pour the hot syrup onto the egg whites and continue to whisk for 30 seconds, or until you have a glossy mixture. Fold in the chocolate mixture then spoon it into the ramekins.

◆ Put the remaining 3 amaretti into a bag, crush with a rolling pin, then sprinkle the crumbs onto the mousses.

▼ Since the mousses contain raw eggs, I would not recommend they be served to the elderly, young children and pregnant women.

TO FREEZE **Cover each ramekin with foil or a double layer of cling film.**

TO DEFROST **Serve as a semi-freddo.**

TO FINISH **Remove from the freezer 10 minutes before serving.**

TO SERVE **You may like to hand round a jug of pouring cream.**

❄ HOT CHOCOLATE SOUFFLES

Little hot chocolate soufflés are the ultimate in puddings: they manage to be both indulging and gutsy whilst retaining a great deal of sophistication. I am a great believer in chocolate puddings tasting of chocolate and the addition of chocolate chips, which melt into the mixture as it cooks, certainly achieves that. Use the type of chocolate chips that are sold for cooking and baking.

   For these soufflés I use large ramekins – mine hold 150ml/5fl oz – and fill them nearly to the top. Cook them from frozen and they will emerge from the oven beautifully risen with lovely wobbling tops.

SERVES 8

butter for greasing

100g/3$\frac{1}{2}$oz very best quality plain chocolate

25g/1oz cornflour

300ml/10fl oz milk

75g/2$\frac{3}{4}$oz sugar

5 egg whites

3 egg yolks

50g/1$\frac{3}{4}$oz plain chocolate chips

TO FINISH

icing sugar

Generously grease 8 ramekins with the butter.

◆ Melt the chocolate, either in the microwave or in a bowl set over a pan of boiling water. Stir until it is smooth then set aside.

◆ Mix the cornflour to a smooth paste with a little of the milk, then stir in 50g/1$\frac{3}{4}$oz of the sugar and the rest of the milk. Pour into a saucepan and, stirring constantly, bring to the boil. Let it bubble gently for a minute, remove from the heat then stir in the chocolate and leave to cool on the side until tepid. Stir the mixture from time to time as it cools to prevent a skin forming.

◆ Whisk the egg whites until stiff, add the remaining sugar and continue whisking for a few moments until you have a glossy meringue mixture.

◆ Stir the egg yolks into the cooled chocolate mixture, then add the chocolate chips. Loosen the mixture by stirring in a large spoonful of the meringue and then fold in the rest of the meringue. Spoon the mixture into the prepared ramekins. I find that the soufflés rise better if you dollop the mixture into the centre so that you end up with a rounded top and clean sides.

TO FREEZE **Cover with foil or a double layer of cling film.**

TO DEFROST **Cook from frozen.**

TO MICROWAVE **Not suitable.**

TO COOK **Heat the oven to 190°C/ 375°F/gas 5 and cook the frozen soufflés for 30–35 minutes when they will be well risen and browning on the top. They should still be slightly liquid in the middle.**

TO FINISH **Sieve a little icing sugar over each one and serve immediately.**

TO SERVE **Hand round a jug of cream or, even better, cream laced with a little brandy, to pour into the centre.**

❋ COFFEE DELICE

This pudding of coffee-flavoured cream layered with biscuits is best eaten very cold, even before it is completely defrosted. I like to make it with a plain biscuit such as Rich Tea or Petit Beurre but you can use sponge fingers. Serve quite small slices as it is rich.

SERVES 6–8

150g/5¹⁄₂oz unsalted butter

150g/5¹⁄₂oz icing sugar

3 eggs, separated

1 tablespoon instant coffee

300ml/10fl oz coffee, made with 1¹⁄₂ teaspoons instant coffee

about ³⁄₄ packet Rich Tea finger biscuits, or similar

TO FINISH

handful split almonds

Grease a loaf tin, or something similar, well and line the base with silicone paper. It won't matter if the paper comes up over the sides or the ends.

◆ Cream the butter and sugar together then add the egg yolks and the instant coffee, dissolved in 1 tablespoon of water, and mix them in well. You can do all this in a food processor. Whisk the egg whites until stiff and fold them into the mixture then spread a spoonful or so of the mixture over the base of the prepared tin.

◆ Pour some of the coffee onto a plate, one by one dip in the biscuits and use them to cover the layer of butter and egg mixture. Spoon some more of the mixture over the biscuits and repeat this operation until you have 3-4 layers of biscuits (depending on the size of the dish). Spread the remaining butter and egg mixture evenly over the top.

▼ Since this dessert contains raw eggs, I would not recommend it be served to the elderly, young children and pregnant women.

TO FREEZE **Cover with foil or with 2–3 layers of cling film.**

TO DEFROST **Defrost for 1 hour in the fridge, then, and this needs to be done when the pudding is still half frozen, turn it out onto a plate and peel off the silicone paper. Leave, refrigerated, for no more than 2 hours longer.**

TO MICROWAVE **Not suitable.**

TO FINISH **Toast a handful of split almonds and sprinkle them over the pudding just before serving.**

❄ RASPBERRY AND REDCURRANT JELLIES

These jewel-like jellies make a lovely sharp and fresh-tasting end to a rich meal. Gelatine can disintegrate if kept frozen for any length of time, but these little jellies keep perfectly for a week or two.

SERVES 6–8

600g/1lb 5oz fresh raspberries

350g/12oz fresh redcurrants

150g/5¹⁄₂oz sugar

1 lemon

6 sheets leaf gelatine

TO FINISH

300ml/10fl oz double cream or double cream mixed with yoghurt

Almond Tuiles (page 132) or biscuits

Put the fruit and 150ml/5 fl oz water into a heavy-bottomed pan, heat gently and simmer for 3-4 minutes. Strain, reserving the juice.

◆ Return the fruit to the pan with another 150ml/5 fl oz water, heat again and simmer for a further 3-4 minutes then strain, again reserving the juice. Repeat once more, this time squashing every drop of juice from the fruit before discarding the debris.

◆ Measure the juice and, if necessary, add water to make it up to 800ml/1¹⁄₃ pints. Stir in the sugar and the juice of ¹⁄₂ the lemon. Taste and add more sugar and/or lemon juice if it needs it. Soak the gelatine in cold water for 5 minutes, drain then add to the hot juice, stirring to dissolve the leaves.

TO FREEZE **Pour the mixture into 6–8 sturdy glasses or ramekins and cover each with foil or a double layer of cling film.**

TO DEFROST **Leave on the side for 3–4 hours or in the fridge for 5–6 hours.**

TO MICROWAVE **Not suitable.**

TO FINISH **Flood the top of each glass or ramekin with a layer of cream, or cream and yoghurt, and, if desired, add a biscuit or Almond Tuile on the side.**

❄ PEARS IN WINE WITH GINGER

Pears in wine has long been a favourite winter pudding. and is well known to be freezer-happy. Flavoured with ginger, this version is especially warming and good on a cold evening.

SERVES 6

6 pears

¹⁄₂ lemon

150g/5¹⁄₂oz granulated sugar

600ml/1 pint fruity white or rosé wine

2 tablespoons ginger wine

1 tablespoon syrup from the stem ginger jar

3 knobs stem ginger, chopped

TO FINISH

crème fraîche or whipped cream

Peel the pears, leaving on the stalk, and rub with the cut side of the lemon to stop them discolouring. Cut a slice off the base of each one and then remove the core with a small sharp knife.

◆ Put the sugar and 600ml/1 pint water in a deep pan that will hold the pears snugly. Heat, stirring until the sugar has melted, then add the wine and the pears. Half cover the pan and simmer the pears for 15-30 minutes, depending on ripeness, or until tender. If the pears are not totally covered by the syrup turn them once during cooking.

◆ Lift out the cooked pears and transfer to a rigid freezer container. Add the ginger wine and syrup to the juices in the pan and bring to a rolling boil. Boil until it has reduced by half to two-thirds, then stir in the chopped knobs of stem ginger and pour it over the pears.

TO FREEZE **Leave until cold then cover the box.**

TO DEFROST **Leave in the fridge for 18 or up to 24 hours.**

TO MICROWAVE **Not suitable.**

TO FINISH **Spoon the syrup over the pears.**

TO SERVE **Serve with a bowl of crème fraîche or whipped cream.**

PEARS IN WINE WITH GINGER

❄ CREPES SUZETTE

I always think of Crêpes Suzette as a naughty and flirtatious pudding and indeed there is one story that it was invented in 1896 at the Café de Paris in Monte Carlo and set before the Prince of Wales and his companion, who was called Suzette. However the chef who laid claim to this invention was only a child at the time and it is known that at about the same time it was a speciality of a well-known Paris restaurant, Chez Marie, so the origin and identity of Suzette remains a mystery. Nowadays the pancakes are nearly always made with orange juice and flavoured with orange liqueur but originally they were made with tangerines which I think would be lovely – you could always try it.

This recipe is simple and rather than heating the crêpes in a frying pan I suggest they are frozen in a shallow gratin dish and then quickly reheated in a hot oven. You can, if you wish, flame them just before serving them, but it won't make that much difference to the taste. Escoffier never did, as he thought they were better without the final drama.

SERVES 6

FOR THE PANCAKES

150g/5^1/$_2$oz flour

2 eggs plus 1 egg yolk

2 teaspoons sugar

pinch salt

zest 1 orange

300ml/10fl oz milk mixed with 125ml/4fl oz water

25g/1oz melted butter plus extra butter for frying

FOR THE FILLING

150g/5^1/$_2$oz unsalted butter

125g/4^1/$_2$oz icing sugar plus extra for sprinkling

zest 1 orange

2 tablespoons orange juice

3 tablespoons Grand Marnier or other orange liqueur

TO FINISH

icing sugar

3 tablespoons Grand Marnier, brandy or orange liqueur

Start by making the batter. Put the flour, eggs and egg yolk, sugar, salt and orange zest into a food processor. Start the machine and pour in the milk and water through the feed tube. When it is mixed and smooth pour in the melted butter. Pour the mixture into a jug and refrigerate for 1 hour or so before making the pancakes.

◆ Using a 18cm/7in frying pan, make the pancakes following the instructions for Asparagus-Filled Pancakes (page 30). You will need 12 for this recipe but any extras can be frozen and used later.

◆ Make the filling by whizzing 125g/4^1/$_2$oz of the butter and the sugar together in a food processor. Add the orange zest and, with the machine running, slowly pour in the orange juice and finally add the liqueur.

◆ Butter a good-sized shallow freezer- and ovenproof dish well and sprinkle on some sugar. Take 12 pancakes and spread some of the filling over each one. Fold each pancake in half and then into quarters and arrange them, overlapping, in the dish. Melt the remaining butter and brush over the top of the pancakes.

TO FREEZE **Cover with foil or a double layer of cling film.**

TO DEFROST **Leave on the side for 5–6 hours or in the fridge overnight.**

TO MICROWAVE **Follow your microwave instructions to defrost the pancakes and, if wished, reheat. Finish as below.**

TO REHEAT **Cover the dish with foil and heat in the oven at 200°C/400°F/gas 6 for 20–25 minutes or until the pancakes are very hot.**

TO FINISH **Sprinkle with icing sugar and the liqueur but if you are going to flame them, warm the liqueur and, with the dish on a steady surface, pour it over and very carefully set light to it.**

TO SERVE **Serve with a jug of cream.**

❄ MASCARPONE TARTE AU CITRON

With its crispy pastry and smooth, rather sharp filling, *tarte au citron* is always a favourite ending to a meal. I find that using mascarpone instead of the more usual double cream gives the filling an especially good taste. The slow cooking gives the tart a creamy consistency and a texture that holds its shape when sliced.

SERVES 6

FOR THE PASTRY

150g/5½oz plain flour

pinch salt

25g/1oz icing sugar

zest 1 lemon

85g/3oz cold unsalted butter, cubed

1 egg yolk

iced water

egg white, lightly beaten for brushing

FOR THE FILLING

250g/9oz mascarpone

zest 2 lemons and 150ml/5fl oz lemon juice (juice 3–4 lemons)

2 eggs plus 2 egg yolks

150g/5½oz caster sugar

TO FINISH

icing sugar

To make the pastry, put the flour, salt, icing sugar and lemon zest in a food processor and process to mix and aerate them. Add the butter and process until the mixture resembles crumbs. Add the egg yolk and 1 tablespoon of iced water and process until the pastry forms a ball. If after 30 seconds the pastry is still crumbly add a little more iced water. Take the pastry from the processor, roll it into a ball, wrap it in foil or cling film and refrigerate for ½ hour. Roll out the cold pastry and use it to line a 23cm/9in tin, leaving a little standing above the rim. Prick the bottom lightly with the tines of a fork and return the prepared pastry case to the fridge for 15 minutes.

◆ Heat the oven to 200°C/400°F/gas 6 and put in a baking tray. Line the tart with foil and weight it with ceramic beans, rice or dried beans and bake for 20 minutes or until just coloured. Remove the foil and beans, turn the oven down to 180°C/350°F/gas 4 and cook for a further 10-12 minutes or until the base is crisp and lightly golden. Take the tart from the oven and immediately brush over the inside with a little lightly beaten egg white. This helps to keep the pastry crisp when the filling is added.

◆ Make the filling by combining all the ingredients in a food processor and whizzing until smooth then pour into the pastry case.

◆ Turn the oven down further to 150°C/300°F/gas 2. Cook for about 30 minutes or until the filling is firming round the edge when the tart is gently shaken. Turn off the oven and leave the tart for a further 20-30 minutes.

▼ To avoid spilling the filling as you lift the tart into the oven to cook it, first rest a baking tray on an oven shelf then pour the filling, or as much as will fit, carefully into the flan then slide the tray neatly in.

TO FREEZE **When cold open freeze the tart then wrap carefully in a large plastic bag and store making sure nothing is on top of it.**

TO DEFROST **Remove from the freezer and leave on the side for 4–5 hours or in the fridge for 10–12 hours.**

TO MICROWAVE **Not suitable.**

TO REHEAT **Serve the tart cold or I prefer it just warmed for 20 minutes in a low oven.**

TO FINISH **Gently sift some icing sugar over the top.**

❄ FRESH APRICOT GALETTE

This pudding uses those delicious downy soft and beautifully coloured fresh apricots and therefore needs to be made in the summer. However, later in the fruit season you could make it with nectarines or use plums which perhaps won't have quite the magic but will still be pretty good.

The galette is made with a large circle of pastry which is drawn up in loose folds round the filling to give it a nice informal look. Under the apricots is a layer of ground almonds and breadcrumbs which not only tastes good but does the job of absorbing any excess moisture from the fruit. I like to use flaked almonds and to grill or fry them to a golden colour before grinding them down in a food processor but it is fine to use bought ground almonds.

SERVES 6–8

FOR THE PASTRY

225g/8oz plain flour

50g/1³/₄oz caster sugar

pinch salt

125g/4¹/₂oz cold unsalted butter, cubed

1 egg yolk

a little cold water

FOR THE FILLING

75g/2³/₄ flaked or ground almonds

25g/1oz fresh white breadcrumbs

75g/2³/₄oz sugar

1kg/2lb 4oz ripe apricots

FOR THE GLAZE

2–3 tablespoons apricot jam

These instructions are for making the pastry in a food processor, but if you don't have one use the hand method. Put the flour, sugar and salt into the bowl and process briefly to mix and aerate them, then add the butter and process until the mixture resembles crumbs. Add the egg yolk and 1 tablespoon of cold water and process until the pastry clings together and forms a ball. You may need to add a little more water.

◆ Turn the pastry onto a board and knead it lightly. Wrap it in cling film and refrigerate for at least 30 minutes.

◆ Take the cold pastry from the fridge. Roll it into a large circle, of about 33-35cm/13-14in in diameter. Transfer it to a baking tray (no matter if it climbs up the sides a little), cover the pastry with a piece of cling film or clean tea towel and refrigerate for a further ¹/₂ hour.

◆ If using flaked almonds grill or dry-fry them until brown. Put the almonds, flaked or ground, into the food processor with the breadcrumbs and 25g/1oz of the sugar and process until everything is very finely chopped.

◆ Spread the almond mixture over the pastry, leaving a 5cm/2in border all round. Halve and stone the apricots and arrange them, cut side down, over the mixture. Sprinkle on the remaining sugar then bring up the sides of the pastry, folding it and curving it over the edge of the outer ring of apricots. When finished the pastry looks rather like an upside down mob cap.

◆ Heat the oven to 200°C/400°F/gas 6, cover the galette loosely with foil and put it into the oven. Remove the foil after ¹/₂ hour and cook for a further ¹/₂ hour or until the pastry is golden and the apricots soft.

◆ Heat the apricot jam and use to glaze the apricots.

▼ To prevent the pastry from cracking when first removed from the fridge leave it on the side for 10 minutes or cut it into cubes and feed them one by one into the running food processor. The pastry will form a ball and should then be easy to roll out while it is still cold.

TO FREEZE **Wrap the galette in foil or cling film.**

TO DEFROST **Leave on the side for 5–6 hours or in the fridge overnight.**

TO MICROWAVE **Not suitable.**

TO REHEAT **The galette is best eaten warm rather than hot so put the defrosted galette into a warm oven, 160°C/325°F/ gas 3, for 20 minutes.**

TO SERVE **Hand round cream in a jug.**

❄ TARTES AUX POMMES WITH CHOCOLATE PASTRY

When I was a child my grandmother always finished off a picnic by giving us a juicy apple and a few squares of dark chocolate. It's a combination I've always remained faithful to.

Sweet pastry is notoriously difficult to roll out but if you make it with a second whizz in a food processor, it should be trouble-free. The recipe makes quite a lot of pastry, especially if you roll it out thinly, but as it is difficult to cut an egg in half I sugggest you make the quantity I give and use any left over to line a small quiche tin, which can be baked and kept until needed in the freezer. For this recipe I use individual loose-bottomed tins with a diameter of 12cm/4¹⁄₂in but you could otherwise use a 25cm/10in quiche tin.

SERVES 6

FOR THE PASTRY
200g/7oz flour
40g/1¹⁄₂oz caster sugar
25g/1oz cocoa
150g/5¹⁄₂oz unsalted butter, cubed
1 egg

FOR THE FILLING
650g/1lb 7oz bramley apples
100g/3¹⁄₂oz caster sugar
75g/2³⁄₄oz butter

FOR THE TOPPING
2 golden delicious apples
4 tablespoons apricot jam
25g/1oz butter
1–2 tablespoons caster sugar

The easiest way to make the pastry is in a food processor. Put the flour, sugar and cocoa into the bowl and pulse the machine a few times to mix and aerate them. Add the butter and process until the mixture resembles fine breadcrumbs. Whisk up the egg, pour it over the mixture and process until the pastry forms a ball. If it doesn't cling together after 30 seconds sprinkle on a little cold water. Mould the pastry into a ball and refrigerate for 1 hour.

◆ Take the cold pastry from the fridge, cut it into cubes and return it to the food processor. Process until it amalgamates, take from the bowl and cut the pastry into 6 more or less even-sized pieces, if using individual tins, and roll each one into a ball. On a floured board, roll out each one into a thin circle and use to line the tart tins. Put the tins back into the fridge for a further ¹⁄₂ hour.

◆ Heat the oven to 190°C/375°F/gas 5. Line each tin with foil, weight it with ceramic beans and bake for 15 minutes. Remove the foil and beans and return the tins to the oven for a further 5 minutes or until the pastry is crisp.

◆ To make the filling, peel and core the bramley apples, cut into chunks and put them into a pan with the sugar, half the butter and 175ml/6 fl oz water. Simmer, stirring occasionally, until very soft. You may need to add some more water. Mix the remaining butter with the hot apple until you have a smooth purée. Cool, then spoon the apple purée into the pastry cases, leaving room for the apple slices.

◆ Peel, core and slice the golden delicious apples. Arrange the slices on top of the bramley purée. Melt the apricot jam, sieve it and stir in the butter. Brush it over the apple slices then sprinkle with sugar.

◆ Bake at 160°C/325°F/gas 3 for 25 minutes or until the apple slices are soft. Leave until cold.

TO FREEZE **Wrap in freezer bags.**
TO DEFROST **Leave on the side for 7–8 hours or in the fridge for 16–18 hours.**
TO MICROWAVE **Not suitable.**
TO FINISH **Best served at room temperature.**
TO SERVE **Hand round a jug of cream.**

❄ MAPLE SYRUP AND PECAN TART

Maple syrup and pecan nuts are a well-tried and very good combination. This tart has a biscuit and nut crust and is filled with a light mousse made from the syrup combined with eggs and cream.

SERVES 6–8

75g/2³/₄oz pecan nuts

10 digestive biscuits

25g/1oz demerara sugar

pinch salt

75g/2³/₄oz butter, melted

3 leaves gelatine

3 egg yolks

200ml/7fl oz maple syrup

150ml/5fl oz double cream

1 egg white

1 tablespoon caster sugar

TO FINISH

icing sugar

handful pecan nuts, halved

Start by making the crust. In a food processor roughly chop the nuts then put in the biscuits, sugar and a pinch of salt. Reduce it all to fine crumbs. Add the melted butter and process briefly to mix. Press the biscuit mixture firmly into the base and up the sides of a 23-25cm/9-10in flan tin, making as neat an edge round the top as you can. This can be quite fiddly and will take a few minutes, but it will eventually come together.

◆ Bake at 190°C/375°F/gas 5 for 6-8 minutes or until the biscuit is a light golden brown. Leave to cool.

◆ Soak the gelatine leaves in a little cold water. Put the egg yolks and syrup into a double boiler or use a good-sized bowl set over a pan of simmering water. Use an electric whisk to whisk until the mixture has thickened. Drain the gelatine, add the leaves to the egg mix and continue whisking until the gelatine has melted and been incorporated. Cool the mixture quickly by putting the pan or bowl in a basin with enough cold water to come at least halfway up the sides. Stir gently from time to time to stop the outside setting while the centre is still warm.

◆ Whisk the cream until thick. Clean and dry the whisk, then, in a separate bowl, whisk the egg white until stiff, add the sugar and whisk again. When the syrup mixture has thickened and is just about to set, whisk the cream into it again using the electric whisk. Finally, using a metal spoon, fold in the egg white. Pour the mixture into the baked crust.

▼ When melting the gelatine, I find it is quicker if the base of the bowl is just immersed in the water.

TO FREEZE **Open freeze the tart, keeping it level. When it is fully frozen, cover with foil or a double layer of cling film and return it to the freezer.**

TO DEFROST **Leave for 5–6 hours on the side or in the fridge overnight. It is best eaten cold, direct from the fridge.**

TO MICROWAVE **Not suitable.**

TO FINISH **Sprinkle a little icing sugar over the tart and decorate with pecan nuts.**

❄ POLENTA, ALMOND AND ORANGE CAKE

Polenta gives cake an interesting slightly gritty texture and, mixed with almonds and orange, it makes a perfect dessert cake. It is not one that benefits from any sort of icing or sweet creamy filling but it looks nice lightly dusted with icing sugar and served with a large bowl of crème fraîche. I quite often serve it with a salad of freshly sliced oranges and if you don't have time to make this at the last minute it too can be made ahead and frozen for a few days.

SERVES 6–8

100g/3¹/₂oz polenta plus 1 spoonful to dust the cake tin

zest and juice 2 large oranges

150g/5¹/₂oz almonds

1 teaspoon baking powder

150g/5¹/₂oz caster sugar

2 eggs plus 1 egg yolk

150g/5¹/₂oz unsalted butter, cubed and softened

TO FINISH

icing sugar

Butter and line the base of a 20cm/8in cake tin and shake a spoonful of polenta around it, discarding any excess. Heat the oven to 160°C/325°F/gas 3.

◆ Pour the orange juice into a pan and slowly bring to the boil. Let it simmer for 10 minutes or so or until it has concentrated and reduced to around 100ml/3¹/₂fl oz. Keep until needed.

◆ Put the almonds and a spoonful of the polenta into a food processor and process until the almonds are ground. Add the remaining dry ingredients and process to mix. Add the eggs, butter and orange zest and juice and process briefly. Scrape down the sides and then use the pulse button a few times to mix everything. Transfer the mixture to the prepared tin and bake for about 40 minutes or until the top is brown. Leave for 5 minutes then turn out onto a rack to cool.

TO FREEZE **Wrap the cake in foil.**
TO DEFROST **Defrost at room temperature for at least 4 hours.**
TO MICROWAVE **Not suitable.**
TO FINISH **Dust with icing sugar.**
TO SERVE **Crème fraîche provides the perfect foil for this cake.**

❄ CHRISTMAS TART

Mince pies can be very good but over Christmas, when one can't move without being offered one, I find that they are inclined to be overdone, so as a substitute I came up with this tart. I was thrilled with the result, which is different enough but still very Christmassy and it certainly went down very well with my family and friends.

I like the pastry case made with the chocolate pastry that I use in the recipe for the Tartes aux Pommes (page 151). The filling is made with a ginger, brandy and spice-flavoured French butter icing into which seasonal goodies are stirred - dried cranberries, nuts, crystallised mixed peel and crushed amaretti - to give it extra flavour and body. Food that freezes well is a great bonus over the Christmas period and this certainly does that. After defrosting, the tart can be served at room temperature or it is good slightly warmed in the oven.

SERVES 6

FOR THE PASTRY

200g/7oz flour

40g/1½oz caster sugar

25g/1oz cocoa

150g/5½oz unsalted butter, cubed

1 egg

FOR THE FILLING

75g/2¾oz granulated sugar

3 egg yolks

125g/4½oz unsalted butter, cubed

4 knobs stem ginger and 1 tablespoon syrup from the jar

1 tablespoon brandy

¼ teaspoon each ground cinnamon, ground nutmeg

50g/1¾oz flaked almonds

125g/4½oz amaretti biscuits

75g/2¾oz dried cranberries

50g/1¾oz chopped mixed peel

Make the pastry following the instructions for Tartes aux Pommes on page 151 and use it to line a 23-25cm/9-10in quiche tin.

◆ Heat the oven to 190°C/375°F/gas 5. Line each tin with foil, weight it with ceramic beans and bake for 15 minutes. Remove the foil and beans and return the tin to the oven for a further 5 minutes or until the pastry is crisp.

◆ To make the filling, put the sugar into a small pan with 100ml/3½fl oz water and place over a low heat. Stir until the sugar has dissolved then raise the heat and bring to the boil and boil for 3-5 minutes until the soft ball stage (116°C/240°F) is reached. If it shows any signs of caramelising immediately whip the pan from the heat. Pour the syrup into the bowl of a food processor. Run the machine and, one by one, add the egg yolks and then the butter. Turn the mixture into a bowl and stir in the ginger syrup, the brandy and the spices.

◆ Cut the ginger knobs into small dice, lightly toast the almond flakes either under the grill or, stirring constantly, in a dry frying pan. Crush the amaretti to crumbs in a food processor or place them in a bag and bash it with a rolling pin. Stir the ginger, the almonds, the cranberries, mixed peel and amaretti crumbs into the icing mixture and spoon it all into the prepared pastry case.

TO FREEZE **Cover with foil or a double layer of cling film.**

TO DEFROST **Leave for 6–7 hours on the side or for 14–15 hours in the fridge.**

TO MICROWAVE **Not suitable.**

TO REHEAT **Warm the defrosted tart in the oven at 160°C/325°F/gas 3 for 20 minutes.**

TO SERVE **Serve with whipped cream laced with some brandy.**

TOP: SEVILLE ORANGE CURD AND ALMOND TART (PAGE 156); BOTTOM, FROM LEFT: MAPLE SYRUP AND PECAN TART (PAGE 152), CHRISTMAS TART

❄ SEVILLE ORANGE CURD AND ALMOND TART

I can never resist stopping and drooling through the windows of French pâtisseries at the displays of quite beautifully decorated and finished pastries and gâteaux. Somewhere in the display there is bound to be a *tarte aux amandes*: a sweet pastry case filled with an almond mixture, possibly topped with apricot jam.

In this recipe the apricot jam has been replaced by a hidden layer of Seville orange curd which mingles well with the slightly gooey almond mixture while giving the tart a lift by adding flavour, freshness and sharpness. When Seville oranges are not available you could use ordinary ones then sharpen up the curd with the zest and juice of a lemon.

I tend to make a whole tart and bake it in a deep 25cm/10in quiche tin. However, for a special effect you can make 6 beautiful individual ones. (See photograph on page 155.)

SERVES 6

FOR THE PASTRY

50g/1³⁄₄oz almonds

150g/5¹⁄₂oz plain flour

50g/1³⁄₄oz caster sugar

100g/3¹⁄₂oz cold unsalted butter, cubed

1 small egg

FOR THE FILLING

150g/5¹⁄₂oz almonds

150g/5¹⁄₂oz caster sugar

100g/3¹⁄₂oz unsalted butter

1 egg

6–8 tablespoons Seville Orange Curd (opposite)

Start by making the pastry. Grind the almonds into a food processor, but stop before they are completely smooth. Add the flour and sugar and process briefly to mix them in. Add the butter and process again until the mixture resembles breadcrumbs. In a bowl break up the egg with a fork. Add about two-thirds of the egg and process, adding more of the egg if necessary, until the mixture clings together and forms a ball.

◆ Turn out the pastry and gently form it into a flat disc. Wrap in foil and refrigerate for at least ¹⁄₂ hour.

◆ Roll out the pastry and use to line the quiche tin, using odd scraps to fill in any holes that form. Use a fork to prick the base then refrigerate for a further 20-30 minutes. Line the pastry case with foil and weight it with some ceramic beans or rice.

◆ Preheat the oven to 190°C/375°F/gas 5, and bake for 20 minutes, then remove the weights and foil. Lower the temperature of the oven to 180°C/350°F/gas 4. Return the pastry case and cook for a further 10 minutes or until the pastry is light gold.

◆ Make the filling by processing the almonds until they are fairly finely chopped then add the sugar and process again to mix. Finally add the butter, cut into cubes, and the egg and process until everything has amalgamated.

◆ Spoon enough orange curd over the pastry base to form a generous layer. Top with spoonfuls of the almond mixture. (You will not be able to smooth it out, so just dot small spoonfuls of the mixture all over the top.)

TO FREEZE **Cover with foil or a double layer of cling film.**

TO DEFROST **Leave on the side for 5–6 hours or in the fridge for 10–12 hours.**

TO MICROWAVE **Not suitable.**

TO COOK **Place the defrosted tart in a preheated oven, 180°C/350°F/gas 4, and cook for 25 minutes. If the tart is not completely defrosted it will need to be cooked for a little longer. The filling will have spread, covering any holes, and be bubbling and golden brown. Leave to cool or serve warm.**

TO SERVE **It is superlative with lashings of crème fraîche.**

❄ SEVILLE ORANGE CURD

Curd can be made with nearly all citrus fruit but Seville oranges are especially good. Although home-made fresh curd will only keep for a few weeks in the fridge it freezes perfectly and can be kept for several months.

SERVES 6

juice 5–7 Seville oranges (250ml/9fl oz)

1 tablespoon cornflour

150g/5¹/₂oz granulated sugar

75g/2³/₄oz unsalted butter

4 egg yolks or 3 whole eggs

Squeeze the juice from the fruit. In a small bowl slake the cornflour in 1 tablespoon of the juice.

◆ Put the remaining juice, the sugar and butter into a saucepan, add the cornflour and bring slowly to the boil, stirring constantly. Bubble for a few seconds to thicken the mixture then take from the heat.

◆ In a mixing bowl use a fork to whisk the eggs lightly, then, still whisking, slowly pour in the hot mixture. Check for sweetness and, if liked, add a little more sugar. Return to the pan and heat, stirring, until it thickens and just reaches boiling point. Cool and then pour into plastic freezer containers or jars.

▼ Egg yolks make the nicest curd but if you want something slightly less rich use whole eggs, and reduce the butter.

TO FREEZE **Cover jars with a double layer of cling film.**

TO DEFROST **Leave on the side for 3–4 hours.**

❄ CHEESE STRAWS ⱽ

I think one of the pleasantest and most relaxed ways of rounding off a meal is sitting chatting, nibbling cheese straws and sipping the remains of any red wine after the pudding plates have been cleared away.

MAKES 20–30

200g/7oz plain flour

100g/3¹/₂oz butter, cubed

¹/₂ teaspoon salt

¹/₂ teaspoon mustard powder and/or pinch cayenne (optional)

100g/3¹/₂oz strong cheddar, or another variety, grated

50g/1³/₄oz parmesan, grated

1 egg

Put the flour, butter, salt, mustard powder and cayenne, if using, into the food processor and whizz until the mixture resembles fine breadcrumbs. Add the remaining ingredients and process until the mixture clings together. You may find that you need to add a few drops of cold water.

◆ Turn the pastry into a ball, wrap it in cling film and refrigerate for at least ¹/₂ hour.

◆ Take from the fridge and leave for a few minutes, which helps to eliminate cracking, then roll out thinly. Cut the pastry into straws and bake in a pre-heated oven, 200°C/400°F/gas 6, for 10-12 minutes or until golden. If you want to serve the straws in bundles cut out a few extra long straws and turn them into circles on the baking tray, then slot the straws into them just before serving.

TO FREEZE **Put the cooled straws into rigid freezer containers.**

TO DEFROST **Take the number you need from the freezer and leave on the side for 1 hour or so.**

TO MICROWAVE **Not suitable.**

TO REHEAT **Place the straws in a warm oven for a few minutes before serving.**

Index